THE SPLENDOR O̶ ̶ ̶ ̶ ̶Y

The Splendor of Accuracy

An Examination of the Assertions Made by
Veritatis Splendor

Edited by

Joseph A. Selling *and* Jan Jans

WILLIAM B. EERDMANS PUBLISHING COMPANY
GRAND RAPIDS, MICHIGAN

© 1994 Kok Pharos Publishing House
Kampen, the Netherlands

This edition published 1995
through special arrangement with Kok Pharos by
Wm. B. Eerdmans Publishing Co.
255 Jefferson Ave. S.E., Grand Rapids, Michigan 49503
All rights reserved

Printed in the United States of America

00 99 98 97 96 95   7 6 5 4 3 2 1

Library of Congress Cataloging-in-Publication Data

The splendor of accuracy: an examination of the assertions
made by Veritatis splendor / edited by Joseph A. Selling and Jan Jans.
p.   cm.
Includes indexes.
ISBN 0-8028-6193-8 (pbk.)
1. Catholic Church. Pope (1978-   : John Paul II). Veritatis splendor.
2. Christian ethics — Papal documents. 3. Catholic Church — Doctrines.
I. Selling, Joseph A. II. Jans, Jan, 1954-
BJ1249.S65   1995
241'.042 — dc20   94-46260
                                   CIP

Table of Contents

Introduction

In the several months that have elapsed since the promulgation of the encyclical *Veritatis Splendor*, the papal letter addressed to the bishops of the Roman Catholic Church dated 6 August 1993 and released to the press on 5 October that same year,[1] a reasonable but not overwhelming amount of response and commentary has appeared especially in the religious press and in professional theological journals. Considering the content of this document, which aims to address the most fundamental principles of Roman Catholic moral theology in the post-Vatican II Church, the amount of response it has received is still somewhat surprising. The reasons for this will be a matter of historical evaluation. One could suggest that what *Veritatis Splendor* has had to say is so obvious and universally accepted by Roman Catholic bishops and moral theologians that there is little need for response. One could also suggest, however, that many people in the Church have taken a 'wait and see' attitude toward what John Paul II has written in his latest encyclical.

Some people will say, indeed some already have said, that the only response that we need to give to *Veritatis Splendor* is a simple 'thank you'. We live in a world that seems to be ruled by moral chaos, where no one seems to remember the norms of morality and the laws that govern moral life. It is as if anyone may do anything they choose, perhaps with the only restriction that no one, i.e., no live healthy adult like you and I,

---

1. "Encyclical Letter *Veritatis Splendor* Addressed by the Supreme Pontiff Pope John II to all the Bishops of the Catholic Church Regarding Certain Fundamental Questions of the Church's Moral Teaching." The language of the English translation of *Veritatis Splendor* is not what has come to be understood as sexually inclusive language. The authors of the present volume have attempted to use sexually inclusive language in their contributions. However, for the sake of accurate representation, quotations from the text of the encyclical have been reproduced as literally as possible from the original version of the official English translation. This has sometimes resulted in a text that is somewhat awkward. We hope that the readers understand this editorial decision, based upon a respect for the integrity and accuracy of original texts.

appears to be 'hurt'. To this world, *Veritatis Splendor* has issued a timely message that calls for a restoration of rules for behavior. There *is* a difference between right and wrong, between acts that are commendable and acts that are contemptuous. This is not only something that we all recognize spontaneously, it lies at the very core of our faith, in the revelation of God who gave us the ten commandments as a guideline for living. The first chapter of the encyclical is an extended meditation on the story in Mt 19, on Our Lord's admonition to the 'rich young man [to] keep the commandments'.

We suspect that a significant number of bishops and professional theologians will have a certain sympathy with this position. For upon examination of the relatively few guidelines or rules for behavior that are presented in *Veritatis Splendor*, most of them, not the least the decalogue, are relatively clear and straightforward. To teach that we should not murder, or steal, or lie, that we should remain faithful to our commitments and fulfill our obligations, that we should live in the love of God and neighbor, are all things that are essential to our striving to live as Christians, believers in the gospel and followers of Jesus Christ.

At the same time, one could ask, 'why is it necessary to write an encyclical to say these things?' Has the following of the most basic commandments and rules for human behavior escaped contemporary consciousness to the extent that we need to restate even the most elementary of moral principles? Perhaps the answer to this question is 'yes'. However, responding to this question would take one far afield into cultural history and comparative anthropology. There is, further, no single, consistent answer to such a question that would univocally fit every contemporary situation. Whether South Africa is riding the peek of moral righteousness, having cast off the affliction of apartheid, or Sarajevo has plunged into the pit of moral degradation, having been plagued with a fratricidal war, is hardly the kind of judgment - even the kind of topic - that one might expect a papal encyclical[2] to address.

---

2. Not all papal encyclicals are written for universal circulation throughout the church. A number of encyclicals, some of which have become rather famous, were in fact written and addressed to a very specific group of people or situation. It goes without saying that *Veritatis Splendor*, addressed to all the bishops of the entire church, does not belong to this genre.

This brings us to a central question that needs to be posed to the text of *Veritatis Splendor*, namely whom, or what situation (time, place, people or culture) does the author of this encyclical have in mind? Does this text address real pastoral situations (e.g., the divorce rate in the United States or the number of abortions in Poland)? Or does it address some notion of universal pastors (priests trained in seminaries) who (should) have one set of universal solutions to every conceivable pastoral problem one might face, anywhere, anytime? What is written in *Veritatis Splendor* appears to presume the second scenario, which of course would absorb the first scenario as well.

If this is indeed the case, then we can presume that the best way to interpret what *Veritatis Splendor* says is not from the point of view of the faithful struggling with moral questions but rather from the point of view of the pastors and their educators. According to the encyclical, there is a problem here. "Modern tendencies" and "certain currents of thought" are creeping in and undermining sound doctrine, leading to confusion and even a crisis in the Church. *Veritatis Splendor* itself can be seen as a direct reaction to this state of affairs that takes the twofold approach of pointing out what those "modern tendencies" are and presenting "the principles for the pastoral discernment necessary in practical and cultural situations" (*VS*, 115).

The modern tendencies might be characterized as the introduction of scientific methods, gleaned from the human sciences such as anthropology, sociology, psychology and so forth, that are then applied to the field of sacred theology with the result that a number of traditional positions and conclusions come under the scrutiny of analytical methods. To the extent that the conclusions indicated by these scientific methods were no longer in harmony with the interpretation of the magisterium on some key issues, those alternative conclusions become characterized as a form of dissent from the ordinary teaching of the magisterium.

As a remedy for this situation, the encyclical proposes a model of "pastoral discernment" while at the same time calling upon the bishops of the church to participate in a process of "common discernment" (*VS*, 115). History, however, has taught us that such a process requires input from all of the members of people of God, according to their capacity and vocation. We cannot afford to see this as anything less than an ongoing process, and we cannot economize on the responsibility to take up this task. In the end, we must be careful to interpret *Veritatis Splendor*, not as the last word in a controversy being put to rest, but rather as a call to participate further in the process of discernment, clarifying the issues at hand and making suggestions for the way forward.

Neither the editors nor the contributors to this volume wish or intend that this study be understood as a challenge or a rebuke to the teaching of the magisterium in the encyclical *Veritatis Splendor*. Nor do we hope that it be understood as 'an answer', much less '*the* answer', of non-traditionalist moral theologians to the accusations made in the text of this papal letter. Our intention is rather to respond to the assertions made in the encyclical that give the impression of pointing to serious problem areas in contemporary Roman Catholic moral theology as it is being researched and taught in any number of seminaries, universities and institutions of higher learning.

We expect that our cumulative response to *Veritatis Splendor* will function as little more than a historical footnote which will testify to the fact that as professional Roman Catholic theologians we have taken very seriously what John Paul II has tried to say to us indirectly by addressing the bishops of the Church. We have sought to combine our loyalty to the Church with our loyalty to our professional colleagues in taking note of what we consider to be crucial issues in contemporary moral theology. We know that these discussions will go on and that in the end, guided by the Holy Spirit, it will not be a matter of 'one side' winning at the expense of the 'other side' losing. We are deeply convinced that the current controversy that is highlighted by the encyclical will be resolved by the grace of God in the same way that all previous controversies have been resolved: "... for the praise and the glory of God's name, for the good of the Church and the good of all God's people"

Joseph A. Selling
Jan Jans

May, 1994

The Context and the Arguments of
Veritatis Splendor

Joseph A. Selling

There is no doubt whatsoever that the most important event that occurred in the Roman Catholic Church during the twentieth century was the Second Vatican Council (1962-1965). Perhaps second only to the reforms mandated by the Council of Trent (1545-1563), the accomplishments of Vatican II were fundamental, sweeping, and affecting just about every aspect of the life of the community and its individual members. So great - and necessary - were the reforms brought about by Vatican II that the Roman Catholic Church is still in the process of working out the implications of what had been done and/or mandated by the council. Because of the fundamental nature of some of these reforms, there remains a difference of opinion with regard to what the Council actually did or intended to do. This is a matter of interpretation: interpreting not only the texts (documents) of the council but seeking to understand those texts against the background of the preparatory work, the work in the various commissions, and the debates that took place during the general meetings of the council. Unlike Trent, which, because of the papal bull of Pius IV, *Benedictus Deus* (16 Jan. 1564)[1], never underwent the scrutiny of examination and interpretation, the chances are very good that (the accomplishments of) Vatican II will be discussed and debated for a very long time, perhaps even to the eve of yet another council.

Among the many issues that are currently being examined in reference to Vatican II is the status of moral theology, or as it has come to be known in some circles, christian ethics. Having recognized that the way moral

---

1. According to *Benedictus Deus*, no commentary or interpretation was allowed to be given to any document or decision of the Council of Trent, with the exception of those official explanations provided by the official Vatican sources. In fact, the official "Acts of the Council" of Trent were only published in this century. See Piet Fransen, "A Short History of the Meaning of the Formula 'fides et mores'," *Louvain Studies* 7 (1978-79) 270-301, p. 289.

theology was being 'done' in the Church (taught in seminaries) up until the time just before the council needed to be reexamined, the "Decree on Priestly Formation," *Optatam Totius*, noted that :

> Special attention needs to be given to the development of moral theology. Its scientific exposition should be more thoroughly nourished by scriptural teaching. It should show the nobility of the Christian vocation of the Faithful, and their obligation to bring forth fruit in charity for the life of the world. (*OT*, 16)

Exactly how moral theology needed to be "developed" is a matter of discussion. *That* it needed development is a matter of record. What the council called for clearly included a serious consideration of formulating a scriptural basis for moral life. That basis, however, could not be introduced without affecting the whole of moral theology at its very foundation. The textbooks of moral theology before the council relied principally upon theories of natural law that were guided by a literal reading of the decalogue. It was a morality of law and precept, of norms and rules formulated by the magisterium and by canon law. The renewal of scriptural studies which was itself promoted at Vatican II implied that even moral theology would have to adapt historical and hermeneutical tools to implement the use of scripture as part of its basis. This, in turn, implied substantial methodological changes within the discipline of moral theology itself. Before very long it became evident to at least some experts in the field that what was needed was not merely a *development* of moral theology but a thorough *revision* of the science.

Those who accepted this conclusion and began the work of reconstructing moral theology on the basis of scripture and tradition rather than natural and canon laws, ultimately came to be known as "revisionists". While at the beginning of this project it appeared that most changes that would take place would amount to broadening the basis of fundamentally unchanged conclusions, that is, finding more and better arguments to substantiate the same positions, it soon became evident that the work of revision would go much deeper and would not necessarily support the statements and conclusions found in the classical handbooks. The reasons for this are multiple, but the single, most accessible explanation for the changes that have taken place in the discipline of moral theology since the council is to be found not in consulting the science but in observing the landscape of moral decision making.

First, there are the issues. Contemporary humanity faces issues and questions that the authors of the moral textbooks never even dreamed would be possible. From the development of nuclear weapons and energy to the very latest techniques for 'keeping persons alive', science and technology have raised questions that were not even thinkable fifty years ago. Secondly, there are the tools of analysis. Human and social sciences have progressed nearly as rapidly as the so-called positive or empirical sciences. Insights into psychology and sociology have opened doors into the human psyche and the very decision-making process itself. Anthropology and ethnology have shed light on the construction and evolution of mores, morals and ethical systems. Philosophy and psychology have exposed the intricacies of valuing and value systems that inform decisions that are being made every day. Thirdly, the context of Roman Catholic Christianity within which moral theology is done and practiced itself has gone through profound evolution as a result of the council. One cannot underestimate the significance and the impact of reintroducing scriptural evidence and biblical theology into the whole of the theological enterprise.

The ramifications for the way in which moral theology would be done would have no less of an impact than what would be experienced in systematic theology, ecclesiology and liturgy. Not the least of those ramifications was the datum that Jesus himself was anything but a legalist. Law is made for human persons and not the opposite (Mt 12:1-8; Mk 2:23-28; Lk 6:1-5). Even the commandments may be said to be perfectly contained in the great, all-encompassing mandate to 'love God and love neighbor' (Mt 22:34-40; Mk 12:28-34; Lk 10:25-28). Thus, when the handbooks of moral theology presented ethical living primarily as a matter of keeping the rules, one could not help but get the impression that they were going about it the wrong way.

The Matter of Interpretation

Because most of the moral issues being faced by contemporary persons were evolving so rapidly, because new tools for moral analysis had become available, and because the nature of theology itself had been going through such profound changes in general, moral theology in the post-Vatican II era could never remain what it had been before the council. It was time to take a critical look at what moral theology had been saying. Many felt that it was also time to rebuild and revise its very foundations.

Not everyone agreed with this conclusion. Many felt that the council had been primarily 'pastoral' and not 'doctrinal' in nature and that any 'changes' that might have been suggested were merely a matter of terminology, making the same message more communicable and more understandable. It began to become evident that there were different interpretations about what the council had accomplished with respect to moral theology. The incident that brought this divergence of opinion to a head was the promulgation, in July 1968, of the encyclical of Paul VI on the question of regulating fertility, *Humanae Vitae*.

In the pre-conciliar moral theology textbooks, contraception had been condemned on the basis of an interpretation of what had been called natural law which concluded that since the 'finality' of the act of sexual intercourse was first and foremost procreation, and since contraception of any sort made the attainment of that finality impossible, then contraception must be wrong because it violated a biological law that was present and in force in the human sexual apparatus because God had determined it to be such.

In his encyclical, Paul VI argued that the "tradition" of the church had constantly taught that contraception was wrong. Since he did not feel that he could depart from that "constant teaching" (*HV*, 6), he took a position that somewhat mildly[2] rejected the use of contraception as a morally acceptable option for married couples. Paul VI appealed to theologians to find "better arguments" to substantiate his teaching. Apparently he did not conceive of the task of moral theology to be an independent investigation into the meaning of the moral implications of leading a Christian life in the contemporary world. He rather appeared to understand that the purpose of the discipline was not to be in any way 'creative' or analytical but rather to be supportive and explanatory of what was taught by the magisterium.[3]

---

2. *Humanae Vitae* must be read in comparison with the encyclical *Casti Connubii* of Pius XI in 1930. Whereas Pius XI brands contraception as a "grave sin," Paul VI never mentions the word sin in his evaluation of contraception (*HV*, 14), reserving his observations about 'sin' to the pastoral reflections about why married couples should remain close to the sacraments (*HV*, 25).

3. *HV*, 28: "Beloved priest sons, by vocation you are the counselors and spiritual guides of individual persons and of families. We now turn to you with confidence. Your first task - especially in the case of those who teach moral theology - is to expound the Church's

Regardless of how one feels or thinks about the issues of contraception and *Humanae Vitae*, it is indisputable that a significant number of theologians, priests, even bishops, not to mention the laity, disagree(d) with Paul VI on his teaching about the question. There were clear differences of opinion expressed, however, not only on the issues themselves but on the role of moral theology as well. Those who thought that the science needed to be completely revised were already in the process of rejecting concepts of the 'natural law' that they found to be biological, static, and 'physicalistic'. The promulgation of *Humanae Vitae* merely hastened these conclusions. Those who thought that moral theology only needed to update its vocabulary and to lengthen its list of arguments in support of basically unchanged positions reacted strongly to what they considered to be 'dissenting voices' in the church. From this time forward, there would be two 'camps' of moral theology within the Roman Catholic Church, the 'revisionists' and the 'traditional' moral theologians.[4]

It was not long before the professional discussion about contraception deepened to consider the methodological approach not only to this particular question but to the whole of moral theology itself. Could one make a specifically *moral* judgment about an act-in-itself, viz. contraception, or was it possible to 'suspend' *moral* judgment on particular acts until more information was gathered about the intention of the person performing the action and the circumstances in which the action took place? The first position was the 'traditional' one: there are certain human actions which are evil in themselves (intrinsically) and which therefore can never be performed for any ulterior motive or in any set of circumstances. The second position was put forth by the 'revisionists', albeit in various ways,

---

teaching on marriage without ambiguity. Be the first to give, in the exercise of your ministry, the example of loyal internal and external obedience to the teaching authority of the Church. That obedience, as you know well, obliges not only because of the reasons adduced, but rather because of the light of the Holy Spirit, which is given in a particular way to the pastors of the Church in order that they may illustrate the truth."

4. I very much dislike attaching labels to groups of persons, and especially to individuals. However, some label is necessary here in order to establish a literary shorthand so that we all know what we are talking about. Having been labeled a member of the 'revisionist' school, I have no difficulty with this word. At the same time, I apologize to anyone who identifies their position with what I refer to as 'traditional' but who resents that terminology. I have chosen this term because I believe that it represents what its proponents would consider to be an honor rather than some discredit.

depending upon which author was consulted. 'Revisionism' in Roman Catholic moral theology was not a unified, consistent manner of approach. In what was felt to be the task of rewriting the whole of moral theology, from its method to its conclusions, it would take at least a generation of reflection and discussion to consider and evaluate various approaches to ethical issues. Many held the opinion that there were some actions, such as contraception, which, although one might not want to call them 'good' strictly speaking, could not be condemned in and of themselves as *morally* evil without knowing more about 'what was going on'. How one could justify such an opinion, however, remained a matter of investigation.

Going beyond the single issue discussion, contemporary moral theological discourse within the Roman Catholic Church eventually came to be preoccupied with so-called 'methodological questions'. Most of these discussions would be considered academic, if not esoteric, by the vast majority of the members of the Christian community. The very fact that Roman Catholic moral theology occupied itself with these questions already signaled a departure from textbook morality. 'Method' had hardly been a concern. Subsequently, the discipline had a great deal of 'catching up' to do. Everything from Anglo-saxon utilitarianism to American pragmatism, from transcendental Thomism to the sociology of knowledge, was investigated, applied, and evaluated for its ethical relevance. In many quarters this is still considered an ongoing process. The questions were not what is moral and immoral but rather how does one arrive at making such distinctions in the first place and then how does one apply them to what are in reality very complex ethical issues? These are the questions of 'method'.

The Wider Context

It is a common opinion that the promulgation of *Humanae Vitae* in 1968 brought to a head the issue of divergent opinions about the intention of the council to 'revise' moral theology. Many people will remember that 1968 was a significant year in many other ways. From the invasion of Czechoslovakia by Soviet troops to the student riots in Paris, 1968 was a year that many people feel marked a turning point in Western civilization, giving (new) birth to free speech, feminism, individual and minority rights, and the audacity of individual citizens to disagree with the policies of their government, something in no small way precipitated by the

American war in Vietnam. A social revolution was going on that manifested itself in every corner of life, from the family to the media, from the
classroom to the streets, from the seats of government to the churches. It
seemed like everything was being questioned, not the least of which was
the role of authority.

Some people actually believed that ethicists and moral theologians
participated in what amounted to an evolution in mores that is still going
on in our times. I suspect that, very much like the rest of its history,
christian ethics was following rather than leading this (r)evolution.
Nevertheless, many thought that simply insisting upon the absolute validity
of all moral rules and the need to enforce these rules would restore order
and return things to the way they used to be. In their eyes, too many
moralists were growing soft and overly tolerant, finding ways to justify
behavior that had previously been condemned both socially and ecclesially.
The more radical proponents of this position blamed the council for the
genesis of this situation. The more mainstream critics of 'modern thought'
claimed that the moral theologians who were finding ways of
accommodation for new ways of behaving were misinterpreting what the
council had taught. The proponents of 'revisionism' claimed to be
operating out of a mandate from the council itself. Attempts to return to
the documents of the council did not solve these questions and it became
a matter of interpretation: exactly what was the council attempting to
accomplish?

Had the 'Revisionists' Gone Too Far?

When one considers the differences between pre-conciliar moral textbooks
and the kind of material that was being produced within a decade after the
council, one can appreciate how quickly things at least seemed to be
moving. There is, perhaps, a certain similarity between this situation and
the events prior to another famous encyclical of this century, *Humani
Generis* (1950).

Although theological studies underwent a small renewal at the end of the
last century, the closing years of the pontificate of Leo XIII once again
witnessed the exercise of strong control by Roman authority over what was
felt to be sometimes too 'creative' work being done in the theological
disciplines. While their protestant counterparts pushed ahead in the field

of biblical exegesis, for instance, employing all the available tools of linguistics, hermeneutics (interpretative sciences), historical studies and comparative analyses of texts, literary criticism and archeological verification, Roman Catholic scriptural studies remained 'traditional' and predictable.

In 1943, Pius XII issued his encyclical, *Divino Afflante Spiritu*, that appeared to give the 'green light' to Roman Catholic biblical exegesis. In a sense, the proverbial floodgates were opened as Catholic biblical scholars struggled to catch up with their protestant counterparts. Things moved quickly, and in the period just following the war, exegetical sciences were once again integrated with the rest of the theological disciplines that were rushing ahead to catch up with 'modern times'. It was the time of the *nouvelle theologie*, a time of new thinking, modern thinking, scientific investigations and explanations.

After years of strict supervision and control, Roman Catholic theologians could now speak their opinions and publicly debate fundamental issues of theology and biblical exegesis using the very latest tools of modern research. Previous taboos seem to be lifted as theologians discussed the Mosaic authorship of the first five books of the bible. Did Adam and Eve represent two, unique individual persons, or was it possible to accommodate the theories of evolution into our understanding of the creation story? Did all the events depicted in the bible actually happen, from the flood to the miracles, or were these stories, myths, allegories that needed to be interpreted?

These were heady times and the speculations were stimulating. But while the theologians reveled in plying their trade, employing the newest of scientific findings and continuously updating just about every tradition and traditional theory, Rome began to worry that the discourse that was becoming increasingly public was disturbing the faith of the average Roman Catholic, especially the unschooled and the poorly educated. Regardless of whether what they were doing was scientifically sound or not, many felt that these theologians of the 'new school' were threatening the trust and the faith of the common believer. It was going too far too fast (for the man or woman in the pew) and it had to stop.

On 12 August 1950, Pius XII issued his encyclical, *Humani Generis*, which did exactly that; it stopped the 'new', modern, approach to theology, aimed at incorporating every tool of contemporary science and philosophy, and reinstated a traditional almost literal approach to scriptural, dogmatic and pastoral questions that perhaps the majority of the laity could understand more easily. Some, including myself, would like to interpret these events as an expression of the wish of those in authority to protect the faith of the majority of Catholics. That said, one must ask whether the cure was not worse that the disease. Neither speculation nor the scientific investigation of theological presuppositions came to an end. It merely went underground. The result was that nearly everything that *Humani Generis* stood for was reversed by the close of the Second Vatican Council, fifteen years later. This, of course, did not directly effect the average Catholic who was for the most part unaware of what had been happening in 'intellectual circles'; and the credibility of the magisterium was only slightly damaged in the eyes of those who were eventually 'rehabilitated' at the time of the council.

The parallel (if there is one) with the situation prior to *Humani Generis* could be suggested to be the response to the mandate of the council (at least according to one interpretation) to revise fundamentally the discipline of moral theology. This was followed by a period of experimentation and speculation, a kind of *nouvelle theologie* for christian ethics. That speculation was broadened by the *Humanae Vitae* event that focused attention on the question of authority and moral teaching. At the same time, while an equally profound (r)evolution was going on in so-called secular life that was calling into question just about every moral rule and tolerating an extraordinary range of human behavior, some authorities felt that the time had come do terminate 'speculation' and to return to more traditional, tested and familiar ways of saying and doing things. Once again, the motivation was pastoral, to protect the faith of the majority of Catholics. Once again, however, one needs to ask whether the remedy is being applied in the right place. What is at stake here is not speculative ideas or theoretical concepts but the credibility of the science of moral theology.

Since the council, a significant number of respected Roman Catholic moral theologians, many of whom were already recognized scholars before the council,[5] had been attempting to revise, refine and strengthen their discipline by fundamentally rewriting its most basic presuppositions. It was not that the foundations of classical textbook moral theology were wrong. The problem was that these foundations had not been seriously looked at for four hundred years. It would be inevitable that any change in the foundations would result in a change in some of the conclusions.

That change was needed was almost universally acknowledged. It was senseless to think that one could speak of moral judgment and decision-making without taking into account the findings of contemporary psychology, sociology and philosophy. This was not at issue. The controversial problems raised by revisionism concerned whether the findings of the contemporary sciences about moral development, varied levels of responsibility and the social and cultural foundation of evaluative[6] as well as descriptive knowledge could be brought right back to the very determination of what was right and what was wrong.

Veritatis Splendor *Comes into Being*

Here, then, was the world in which *Veritatis Splendor* came into being. Since the social revolution of 1968 (primarily in what might be called the North Atlantic world of Western Europe and North America), with its emphasis upon freedom and creativity, individual and social experimentation had reached a point where it seemed that most any form of human behavior could find social acceptance, or at least tolerance. The credibility of moral authority had been seriously undermined politically by the Vietnam war and ecclesially by the disputes over contraception. The prosperity and the technological advancement of the 1970's and 1980's had provided a broad cross section of the population with opportunities that had not even been dreamed by the preceding generation. Open education, the affordability of travel, and a commercial atmosphere that was willing to sell anything to anyone created a situation in which 'anything was possible'.

---

5. To name a few of the better known scholars I have in mind, F. Böckle, J. Fuchs, B. Häring, and L. Janssens.

6. The distinction of "evaluative knowledge" is one of the arguments used to understand dissent from the teaching of *Humanae Vitae* by Karl Rahner, "Zur Enzyklika 'Humanae Vitae'," *Stimmen der Zeit* 93 (1968) 193-210, an English version of which can be found in *Catholic Mind* 61 (1968) 28-45.

Simultaneously, the discipline of moral theology had been undergoing its most profound revision since the counter-reformation in the sixteenth century. Not only were particular questions (contraception, conscientious objection, the management of surplus wealth and environmental responsibility) a matter of intense discussion, but the very foundations of ethical thought were being reviewed and even 'revised'. Catholic moral theologians had no doubt that there was such a thing as 'right and wrong', but exactly how one determined what was right and what was wrong was a matter of ardent speculation. What is more, out of a spirit of pastoral concern and a willingness to help individual persons come to grips with serious questions, these same moral theologians were willing to share their speculations with a wider public. To the outside observer[7] it at least could have appeared that moral theology had capitulated to the individualist, consumer, 'anything goes' spirit of the times. When this speculative zeal crossed paths with equally pastorally minded executors of authority over particular issues upon which no agreement seemed possible, there would inevitably be a clash. In the Roman Catholic Christian community, these paths crossed and crisscrossed over the entire area of marriage and human sexuality.[8] In the minds of some responsible and deeply concerned stewards of authority, things had simply gone too far.

In the summer of 1987, John Paul II came to the decision that there was a need to address not simply the current debates that were taking place within the public forum and the church community itself, but the very foundations of morality as a theological discipline. He announced that he would write an encyclical on the topic because he felt that those

---

7. By "outside observer" I mean anyone who did not follow the development of moral theology with a professional understanding. This would apply to theologians who were not specifically trained in that field or to non-theologians, such as philosophers who knew a good deal about natural law theory or legal philosophy but relatively little about theological concepts such as grace (fundamental option), covenant (biblical theology, the meaning of sin as a theological concept) or pastoral care (diminished guilt, internal forum, material sin, or the lesser evil solution to moral dilemmas).

8. Sexual ethics is here singled out because it constitutes the most obvious and public area of moral debate within the Catholic Church. It should not be thought, however, that this is the only area in which there is disagreement and divergence. Topics like the economic structure of the western world, the use of (military) force to solve political problems and the level of environmental responsibility versus the interests of capital investment are also matters of intense ethical debate.

foundations were being undermined by certain contemporary theories.[9] It took six years, and if rumors could be believed several drafts, for this encyclical to be published. In it one finds not only the reflective words of the Bishop of Rome but evidently as well the counter-(r)evolutionary speculations of theorists representing the more traditional school of christian ethics.[10]

The first and the last of the three chapters that constitute the encyclical reflect much more literally the thought and style of John Paul II. The first chapter (*VS*, 7-27) is primarily an extended meditation or homily on the story of the person who approaches Jesus to ask "what good must I do to have eternal life?" (Mt 19:16).[11] The third chapter (*VS*, 84-117) is concerned with authority and discipline in the church. However, the second chapter, dedicated to the development of moral theory and argumentation, is a highly technical text that reflects, and in my opinion could not have been written without a thorough knowledge of, the literature which has been appearing in the professional theological journals over the past twenty years. It is inevitable that one will speculate about who is behind this text. For the moment, we will simply point out some of the persons who are evidently the foremost candidates for criticism in the minds of the author(s) of this chapter.

The Unnamed Authors

A number of commentaries on *VS* have noted that although the encyclical alleges to single out particular trends in contemporary Roman Catholic

---

9. The Apostolic Letter *Spiritus Domini* (1 August 1987) was addressed to the moderator of the Redemptorist order on the occasion of the second centenary of the death of St. Alphonsus de Liguori, *A.A.S.* 79 (1987) 1365-1375.

10. See Joseph A. Selling, "Ideological Differences: Some Background Considerations for Understanding *Veritatis Splendor,*" *The Month* 255 (1994) 12-14.

11. An investigation of the use of scripture in the encyclical is dealt with by Gareth Moore elsewhere in this volume. I will therefore not treat this and the parallel passages further here, except to note that in my opinion the principal point of the story of 'the rich young man' is not about (keeping) the commandments at all but actually about the insufficiency of such an approach to enter into discipleship: "one thing you still lack" (Lk 18:22b). See Joseph A. Selling, "*Veritatis Splendor* and the Sources of Morality," *Louvain Studies* 19 (1994) 3-17, pp. 7-9.

moral theology, no individual authors are named. While that may be the case, it is equally evident to someone familiar with the literature that the author(s) of this text had particular individuals in mind. The use of certain approaches, even certain words, can identify an individual author whose contribution to moral theology is associated with a given method or terminology. Some of these references are more obvious than others, and not all of them are negative. At this point, I will avoid drawing attention to those authors whom I believe inspired the text (of the second chapter) in the first place, primarily those associated with the 'basic goods theory' (*VS*, 51).

Three general references in *VS* indicate a familiarity with terminology that, although 'originally' associated with a particular author have come to be so widely discussed that the actual source could have come from many places. The first is to the concept of "autonomy". The entire discussion of "Freedom and Law" (*VS*, 35-51), the first subdivision of the second chapter, appears to be obsessed with this idea, although mention is never made of the theologian who is most often associated with the notion in Roman Catholic circles. This, of course, is Alfons Auer whose well known book on autonomy sparked a lively debate among Catholic moral theologians.[12] The second such reference is to the even more generally spoken of concept of the "fundamental option", a topic that was brought to the fore in Catholic discussion mainly through the work of Bernard Häring. While other names are also associated with the concept in the post-conciliar period, especially those of Karl Rahner, Herman Reiners, Josef Fuchs and Piet Fransen, it was Häring who brought it onto center stage through his numerous (including popular) works and the follow-up to his original three volume masterpiece which bears the title *Free and Faithful in Christ*.[13] The theory of the fundamental option puts an entirely

---

12. Alfons Auer, *Autonome Moral und christlicher Glaube* (Dusseldorf: Patmos, 1971). The second edition (1984) of this work includes a summary of the criticisms of the first edition as well as Auer's response to those criticisms. So far as I know, this text has never been translated into English.

13. Häring's monumental achievement in the 1950's was his three volume work, *Das Gesetz Christi: Moraltheologie, dargestellt für Priester und Laien* (Freiburg: Wewel, 1954). This was not published in English until ten years later as, *The Law of Christ: Moral Theology for Priests and Laity* (Westminster: Newman, 1964). *Free and Faithful in Christ: Moral Theology for Priests and Laity* (Slough: St. Paul) was published simultaneously with the

different light on the concept of sin than that reflected in the moral handbook approach to sin as an isolated, individual, a-historical, and a-contextual act. In the handbooks, sin is equivalent to breaking or failing to fulfill a rule or law. Through his ground-breaking work on the *Law of Christ* in which morality was seen not as something static and legislative but something dynamic and vocational, Häring laid the foundation for reinterpreting the concept of sin in Roman Catholic thought. His adaptation of the theory of fundamental option gave not only credibility but rationality to his approach that has had a lasting influence in the discipline.

A third general reference could be suggested with respect to what *VS*, 37 calls "a sharp distinction, contrary to Catholic doctrine, between an *ethical order* ... and an *order of salvation."* This appears to refer to some of the work of Josef Fuchs who indeed does distinguish between moral truths and the truths of salvation, but who certainly does not insinuate any "sharp distinction" between these as the encyclical so indicates.[14]

Three more general references do not rivet the attention of the casual reader because they appear to be detectable only through the use of particular words. The first is to the concept of "theonomy" or "participated theonomy" (*VS*, 41) that is generally ascribed to Franz Böckle.[15] This concept is passed over rather quickly and positively in the encyclical, without drawing attention to what the same author had to say about the structure of moral theology itself. In place of this, one finds the idea being used to 'counteract' the notion of autonomy itself, as if this were a direct and pertinent answer to the writings of Auer. The second terminological reference appears to be to Bruno Schüller and the concept of "paraenesis" with respect to norms found in divine revelation.[16]

German version, *Frei in Christus: Moraltheologie für die Praxis des christlichen Lebens* (Freiburg: Herder) in 1978-1981.

14. See. Josef Fuchs, "Moral Truths - Truths of Salvation?" in *Christian Ethics in a Secular Arena* (Washington: 1984), pp. 48-67. See below for a fuller discussion of paragraph 37.

15. *Fundamentalmoral* (München: Kosel, 1977); *Fundamental Moral Theology* (Dublin: Gill and Macmillan, 1980).

16. One could consult Schüller's *Die Begründung sittlicher Urteile: Typen ethischer Argumentation in der Moraltheologie* (Düsseldorf: Patmos, 1973, 2n ed. 1980) or his more recent *Der menschliche Mensch: Aufsätze zur Metaethik und zur Sprache der Moral* (Düsseldorf: Patmos, 1982; *Wholly Human: Essays on the Theory and Language of Morality,*

Thirdly, a single-word, but unmistakable reference occurs at the very beginning of the discussion on "The Moral Act" (*VS*, 71-83) when the encyclical
draws attention to the concept of "ontic evil". At first sight, one finds a
discussion of 'teleological' reasoning (that the text describes by coining the
word "teleologism") that is quickly associated with "proportionalism, and consequentialism" (as if these two categories were related to each other). Any
theory of proportionality relies upon some concept of evil that is not (yet)
morally qualified. In most of the literature this is called "non-moral" or "pre-
moral", sometimes even "physical" evil. There is only one author associated
with the development of the concept of "ontic evil" and that is L. Janssens.[17]

Finally, one author who has already admitted to being able to "find
himself" in the pages of the encyclical is Charles Curran. In its discussion
of the "alleged conflict" between nature and freedom (*VS*, 46-48) the
encyclical proposes that some authors "conceive of freedom as somehow
in opposition to or in conflict with material and biological nature." This
is clearly most pertinent in the area of sexual ethics, a domain in which a
great deal of discussion has taken place on the relationship between
biological observations and moral rules. The encyclical then takes up the
"*objections of physicalism and naturalism* [that] have been levelled against
the traditional conception of *the natural law*" such that "according to
certain theologians, this kind of 'biologistic or naturalistic argumentation'
would be present in certain documents of the Church's Magisterium,
particularly those dealing with the area of sexual and conjugal ethics."
These ideas undoubtedly reflect the positions that Curran has taken on the
issues of masturbation, contraception, sterilization and homosexual acts.[18]

Washington: Georgetown University Press, 1986), which unfortunately is not available to me.
The idea of paraenesis being used in fundamental moral theology was introduced to the
English speaking world by Richard A. McCormick in his "Notes on Moral Theology," who
in turn ascribed the idea to Schüller's lectures on the topic at the Gregorianum in 1973. See
Notes on Moral Theology 1965 through 1980 (Washington: Univ. of America Press, 1981)
528.

17. See, for instance, "Ontic Evil and Moral Evil," *Louvain Studies* 4 (1972-1973) 115-156;
and "Ontic Good and Evil, Premoral Values and Disvalues," *Louvain Studies* 12 (1987) 62-
82.

18. See, for instance, Charles E. Curran, *Issues in Sexual and Medical Ethics* (Notre Dame,
Ind.: Univ. of Notre Dame Press, 1977) and *Transition and Tradition in Moral Theology*
(Notre Dame, Ind.: Univ. of Notre Dame Press, 1978).

Although the encyclical does not 'name' specific authors, it is evident that the works, the methods and the terminologies of certain Roman Catholic moral theologians were known to the author(s) of the second chapter. One who is not familiar with the literature would not have been in a position to use terms like autonomous morality, theonomy, paraenesis, ontic evil or physicalism and biologism. One who is not familiar with the technical debates about fundamental option as well as its application to the understanding of sin on a practical as well as theoretical level, could not have composed the technical discussion on that topic. In other words, the author(s) of the second chapter of the encyclical not only had certain ideas in mind but they made a conscious effort to refer to and to refute the writings of particular persons as well. All the moral theologians mentioned here are well known, respected figures in their discipline. When it is suggested therefore, that the author(s) of *VS* had these particular persons in mind, perhaps the most cogent rebuttal that can be given to that suggestion is that the ideas to which I have drawn attention here are present in the writings of numerous scholars. If nothing else, this testifies to the influence, and I would suggest the credibility, of the moral theologians that the encyclical did not name.

Anxiety about Contemporary Trends or Tendencies

Reading the opening paragraphs of the encyclical, one gets a sense of alarm, perhaps even impending doom. "The purpose of the present encyclical" (*VS*, 4), paints a picture of moral disintegration on the level of the most basic principles that are no longer merely matters of "doubts and objections", of "limited and occasional dissent, but of an overall and systematic calling into question of traditional moral doctrine." The root of this "calling into question" is suggested to be the "influence of currents of thought which end by detaching human freedom from its essential and constitutive relationship to truth." The theme of 'freedom and truth' will be a recurrent one throughout the text. However, it is perhaps worth noting here that whatever "currents of thought" are being spoken of, it is only *the end* of these currents that supposedly detach freedom from truth.[19]

---

19. One could also say that it is only a *possible* effect of these 'currents' that might result in such a 'detachment of freedom and truth'. In some places, most notably *VS*, 29, the encyclical evaluates these 'currents' quite positively. It appears that John Paul II is only fearful of some of the possible *consequences* of certain ways of thinking and not necessarily

One still wonders what those currents might be, since they are not named here.

As one reads on, one finds more results or effects of these "currents of thought", ranging from a 'rejection' of the traditional doctrine of the natural law to a questioning of the efficacy of magisterial statements. These effects appear to culminate in a particular question that the encyclical claims is being asked "in Seminaries and in Faculties of Theology", namely "do the commandments of God, which are written on the human heart and are part of the Covenant, really have the capacity to clarify the daily decisions of individuals and entire societies?" (*VS*, 4)

Before going on, one might wonder who is asking this question? The implication seems to be that (even ?) professors of moral theology are engaging in some sort of speculation that could appear to cast doubt on the relevance of the "commandments of God". At this point, however, these "commandments" are not identified. They are said to be "written on the heart", which does not necessarily point immediately to the decalogue. Nevertheless, even those commandments that are "part of the Covenant", and which might specifically point in the direction of the decalogue, are not actually being questioned by anyone. Identifying the question of what might "have the capacity to clarify the daily decisions of individuals and entire societies", it would seem that any responsible professor of moral theology or teacher of ethics would attempt to maximize the sources for clarification rather than eliminate any source, including commandments, without serious consideration.

Returning to the original problem, that there are "currents of thought" which have resulted in certain "trends" or "tendencies" to which the Magisterium feels some duty to respond appears to be both the motivation and the central theme of the encyclical (*VS*, 5 & 27).[20] Indeed, this is the

---

of those ways of thinking themselves.

20. *VS*, 5: "Given these circumstances, which still exist, I came to the decision - as I announced in my Apostolic Letter "Spiritus Domini" issued on 1 August 1987 on the second centenary of the death of Saint Alphonsus Maria de' Liguori - to write an Encyclical with the aim of treating "more fully and more deeply the issues regarding the very foundations of moral theology", foundations which are being undermined by certain present day tendencies." *VS*, 27: "Precisely on the questions frequently debated in moral theology today and with

very title of the second chapter of the document, "The Church and the Discernment of Certain Tendencies in Present-day Moral Theology." Lest one think that what is being undertaken here is merely a matter of fraternal correction, an adjustment of certain speculative theories, the author is quick to point out that,

> ... within the context of the theological debates which followed the Council, there have developed *certain interpretations of Christian morality which are not consistent with "sound teaching"* ... the Magisterium has the duty to state that some trends of theological thinking and certain philosophical affirmations are incompatible with revealed truth. (*VS*, 29)

These are rather serious charges that would seem to warrant our most careful attention. If what is being taught in seminaries and universities is "not consistent with sound teaching" and is "incompatible with revealed truth", it would appear that the church itself is in a state of major crisis.

Still, one is not quite sure exactly what these trends or tendencies might be. A search through the text of the encyclical reveals that the words "trend" or "tendency" occur 15 times in 13 paragraphs[21] Some of these occurrences are merely a repetition of the observation that 'certain trends or tendencies' exist. Others seem to point more clearly toward particular 'tendencies' that break down basically into three categories.

Tendencies of Discernment

The first category of 'tendencies' involves a "novel interpretation" (*VS*, 34) or "creative understanding" (*VS*, 54) of conscience and the relationship

---

regard to which new tendencies and theories have developed, the Magisterium, in fidelity to Jesus Christ and in continuity with the Church's tradition, senses more urgently the duty to offer its own discernment and teaching, in order to help man in his journey towards truth and freedom."

21. "Trend" occurs in *VS* 29, 36, 74, 115; and "tendency/ies" occurs in *VS* 5, 27, 32, 34 (3x), 35, 54, 66, 67, 106. One could also search for the phrase "currents of thought" to identify the concerns of the author of this text. Such a search reveals that the terminology of "currents" occurs roughly in the same places as trends and tendencies: *VS*, 4, 32 (2x), 34, 35, 37, 75.

between freedom and truth (*VS*, 34) or freedom and law (*VS*, 34, 35, 36, 54). This tendency is said to *come under the influence of* - nb: not to be equivalent with - "currents of subjectivism and individualism" (*VS*, 32, 34). The result is a sense of "(moral) autonomy" which would "grant to the individual conscience the prerogative of independently determining the criteria of good and evil" (*VS*, 32), "propose novel criteria for the moral evaluation of acts" (*VS*, 34), or "grant to individuals or social groups the right to determine what is good or evil" (*VS*, 35), so that "human freedom would thus be able to 'create values'" (*VS*, 35) and "human reason exercises its autonomy in setting down laws" (*VS*, 36).

What is at issue here is the role of human reason in the discernment of some of the most fundamental concepts of moral discourse, good (value)[22] and evil, and the subsequent pronouncement of statements that either recommend or dissuade their realization (norms or laws). Note that the concept of "freedom", which is presented as being held in juxtaposition ("alleged conflict") with law and/or truth, and is stereotyped as a *cause* for certain exaggerated claims of reason with respect to law and/or truth, is in fact only the *result* of an understanding of *reason* which is more properly said to be not 'free' but 'autonomous', even before the exercise of freedom is possible. In fact, in only one place does the encyclical lay claim to the identification of freedom and autonomy.

> Human freedom would thus be able to "create values" and would enjoy a primacy over truth, to the point that truth itself would be considered a creation of freedom. Freedom would thus lay claim to a *moral autonomy* which would actually amount to an *absolute sovereignty*. (*VS*, 35)

Every other reference to autonomy is either to "rightful autonomy" or to

---

22. Although most current literature, including statements from the magisterium, use the words 'good' and 'value' interchangeably, I propose that the linguistic distinction actually signifies an important difference between these categories. Whereas the label 'good' may be attached to something on the basis of observation and consultation that is carried out without any particular interest (one can determine that something is worthy of the label 'good' even though one has no interest whatsoever in pursuing or attaining that thing), to say that something is 'valuable' implies a relationship between the person(s) making the statement and the thing being considered. To value something is to be willing to use, even sacrifice, one's resources, time and energy to achieve, hold on to, or increase the thing said to be 'valuable'.

the "autonomy of reason".[23] It should not be forgotten that this same autonomy is considered to be a sign of the dignity of the person created in God's image. The encyclical itself (*VS*, 38) quotes Gregory of Nyssa who wrote,

> The soul shows its royal and exalted character... in that it is free and self-governed, swayed autonomously by its own will. Of whom else can this be said, save a king?... Thus human nature, created to rule other creatures, was by its likeness to the King of the universe made as it were a living image, partaking with the Archetype both in dignity and in name.[24]

Preceding an act of the will (exercise of freedom) is the process of discernment, and this, in turn, takes place through the exercise of reason. The question is, how 'autonomous' is this reason? Even the encyclical takes note of the "rightful autonomy of (the practical) reason" (*VS*, 40). It even recognizes that the "claims of autonomy" have caused Catholic moral theology to undertake a "profound rethinking about the role of reason and of faith in identifying moral norms," and further "acknowledged that underlying this work of rethinking there are *certain positive concerns* which to a great extent belong to the best tradition of Catholic thought." (*VS*, 36)

---

23. Incidental references to the "claims of autonomy" or "concept of autonomy" obviously just introduce something that has been or is about to be said and are therefore non-committal (*VS*, 36, 37, 40), as are the references to the "autonomy of earthly realities" (*VS*, 38, 39; cf. *GS*, 36). The other references are:
[36] the expression of a law which man in an autonomous manner lays down for himself and which has its source exclusively in human reason ... the sense that human reason exercises its autonomy
[37] a generic paraenesis, which the autonomous reason alone would then have the task of completing with normative directives ... an interpretation of the autonomy of human reason
[38] a rightful autonomy is due to every man
[40] The rightful autonomy of the practical reason ... the autonomy of reason
[41] Man's genuine moral autonomy in no way means the rejection but rather the acceptance of the moral law
[55] making these decisions "autonomously"
[61] alleged autonomy in personal decisions

24. Reference given in the text is to *De Hominis Opificio*, Chap. 4: *PG* 44, 135-136.

Yet this very phenomenon would appear to be at odds with the so-called claim of "autonomy", a claim said to be equivalent to a "complete sovereignty of reason" in the discernment of moral norms. The antidote to this is presumably submission to the will of God as the author of the moral law. In a crucial passsage, we read,

> These trends of thought have led to a denial, in opposition to Sacred Scripture (cf. Mt 15:3-6) and the Church's constant teaching, of the fact that the natural moral law has God as its author, and that man, by the use of reason, participates in the eternal law, which it is not for him to establish. (*VS*, 36)

In one sense, this position is very Thomistic. But in another, perhaps more pertinent sense, it departs from what Thomas was attempting to say. If natural law is 'nothing more than the participation of the rational creature in the eternal law',[25] then the very possibility of that participation is the function of reason. One must be careful to distinguish the two, however, lest one get the mistaken impression that even the eternal law is directly knowable by human persons (Cf. *S.T.*, I-II, q. 93, a. 2). Natural law is not only knowable by human persons but it is precisely the vocation of human persons[26] to discern and apply its meaning. Furthermore, the passage cited here creates a certain but real ambiguity by distinguishing between God as the *author* of the "natural moral law" and the one who *establishes* the eternal law. The proximity of these concepts could leave one with the impression that God is responsible for both in exactly the same way. If that were true, there would be no place whatsoever left for the role of reason.

I dwell upon this concept because it points to an extremely significant, if not decisive, theological position: whether human reason is capable of discerning good and evil, right and wrong, independently of Divine Reve-

---

25. Reference is made to Thomas' definition of natural law (*S.T.*, I-II, q. 91, a. 2) three times in the encyclical at notes 19 (*VS*, 12), 76 (*VS*, 42) and 82 (*VS*, 43); the reference, however, is not given at this passage.

26. Using the term 'human person' here should not leave the impression that we are speaking of individuals. Persons are always persons-in-community. Individuals do not discern truth "all on their own," as it were, but are always dependent upon a community. Cf. *Dignitatis Humanae*, 3.

lation. It is a typically 'Catholic' position to argue from Rom 2:15 that indeed all human persons, whether or not they have the gift of revelation, are capable of knowing good and evil because of the "law written on their hearts". The encyclical refers to this passage three times,[27] but at this point in its argumentation, where it is insinuated that there is no distinction between eternal and natural law, the encyclical comes frighteningly close to overlooking this ancient tradition.

> Some people, however, disregarding the dependence of human reason on Divine Wisdom and the need, given the present state of fallen nature, for Divine Revelation as an effective means for knowing moral truths, even those of the natural order,[62] have actually posited a *complete sovereignty of reason* in the domain of moral norms regarding the right ordering of life in this world. (*VS*, 36)[28]

For our purposes here, we will ignore the *non sequitur* jump from the ability to know moral truths to positing a "complete sovereignty of reason". We will also disregard the insinuation that a responsible moral theologian would "disregard the dependence of human reason on Divine Wisdom". What we need to draw attention to is the assertion of "the need ... for Divine Revelation as an effective means for knowing moral truths, even those of the natural order." The reference given here (note 62) is to the famous encyclical of Pius XII, *Humani Generis*,[29] in which a similar topic is discussed. In some contrast to this text, Pius XII is careful to point out that in view of our fallen nature it is only for the purpose of achieving *certainty* that our knowledge is freed from error that Divine Revelation is

---

27. Rom 2:15 is indirectly referenced in *VS*, 59, is paraphrased in *VS*, 12, and is quoted as a title at *VS*, 46.

28. On this question, the encyclical is thankfully not consistent. Somewhat later, in *VS*, 74, we read: "Many of the Catholic moralists ... recognize the need to find ever more consistent rational arguments in order to justify the requirements and to provide a foundation for the norms of the moral life. This kind of investigation is legitimate and necessary, since the moral order, as established by the natural law, is in principle accessible to human reason." Other places where the discussion of human reason is carried on but is not always consistent include *VS*, 40, 42, 43, 44, 48, 59, 60, 61, 72 & 79.

29. Pius XII, *Humani Generis* (12 August 1950), *A.A.S.* 42 (1950), 561-578, pp. 561-562.

... man is no longer convinced that only in the truth can he find salvation. The saving power of the truth is contested, and freedom alone, uprooted from any objectivity, is left to decide by itself what is good and what is evil. This relativism becomes, in the field of theology, a lack of trust in the wisdom of God, who guides man with the moral law.[50]

Here, 'relativism' is linked with one of the favorite themes of the second chapter that is always characterized in a radical way, absolute freedom or 'freedom alone'. This freedom is said to be "uprooted from any objectivity" so that what is determined to be good or evil is solely dependent upon some concept of freedom. Apparently there is a dipolarity between 'objectivity' and 'relativism'. This, of course, begs the question of the context and the content of that 'objectivity'. The answer to that question is found earlier, in chapter two.

Faced with this theory,[51] one has to consider carefully the correct relationship existing between freedom and human nature, and in particular *the place of the human body in questions of natural law*. [....]
It is in the light of the dignity of the human person - a dignity which must be affirmed for its own sake - that reason grasps the specific moral value of certain goods towards which the person is naturally inclined. And since the human person cannot be reduced to a freedom which is self-designing, but entails a particular spiritual and bodily structure, the primordial moral requirement of loving and respecting the person as an end and never as

---

50. The reference as it appears in notes 136 & 137 is: *Address* to those taking part in the International Congress of Moral Theology (10 April 1986), 1: *Insegnamenti* IX, 1 (1986), 970-971.

51. The 'theory' being spoken of here is the criticism on the part of 'certain theologians' (i.e., Charles Curran) who raise "objections of physicalism and naturalism" at the root of specific teachings in sexual morality. This topic is exposed (but not answered) in *VS*, 47, which ends with the statement, "The workings of typically human behavior, as well as the so-called "natural inclinations", would establish at the most - so they say - a general orientation towards correct behavior, but they cannot determine the moral assessment of individual human acts, so complex from the viewpoint of situations."
The reaction to this position is found in the next paragraph (quoted here) which falls back upon the medieval concept of natural law.

> a mere means also implies, by its very nature, respect for certain
> fundamental goods, without which one would fall into relativism
> and arbitrariness. (*VS*, 48)

First, considering the "theory" to which a response is about to be given, it
appears that the author of this text considers "typically human behavior as well
as the so-called natural inclinations" to be ethically normative (i.e., determining "the moral assessment existing between freedom and human nature"). The
"natural inclinations" spoken of are seen as pointers for enumerating the
"certain goods" which supposedly enjoy a "specific moral value" that is
grasped by reason and is based not upon freedom but upon "a particular
spiritual and bodily structure." Therefore, even an ethics that claims to be
based upon respect for the human person (personalism?) is predetermined -
"by its very nature" - by "respect for certain fundamental goods."

To summarize even more briefly: natural inclinations (exhibited by typical
human behavior) direct us to certain fundamental goods that possess a
specific moral value and must be respected lest "one would fall into
relativism." Here is the only indication of the meaning of relativism
provided by the encyclical. Ultimately, relativism is not connected with
freedom or laws or conscience or subjectivism or any sort of 'teleologism'. Relativism is the refusal to recognize certain goods as having
inviolable moral value. To respect the person, one must respect "certain
fundamental goods". On the basis of this proposition, one can begin to
understand the tremendous importance that the encyclical places upon the
moral meaning of the *object* of the moral act: regardless of intention or
circumstances, work against, choose between or in any way sacrifice one
of these "fundamental goods" and the action is already morally qualified.

The astute observer will recognize here a form of neo-scholastic natural
law theory, but now taken one step further. In scholasticism, 'inclinations'
were used as an indication for what might be labeled as good (*bonum est,
quod omnia appetunt*). Before a specific individual could respond to that
good in a way that might be classified in some way or another as moral,
however, a number of steps were still necessary, not the least of which
was the specific acknowledgment of that good (*bonum apprehensum*). With
the knowledge of something that might be called good (we would say in
a pre-moral way) one still had to work out the relationship with other
goods as well. Thus, motivated to choose the 'greater good', one was still

free to discard or sacrifice another good, even if it were something that could be recognized as the object of our individual (or even 'collective', i.e., 'natural') inclination(s).

Whereas most of us are comfortable with the use of this word 'good' as an adjective, 'this is good, that is not good', the encyclical exhibits the use of very contemporary (technical) language by using the word as a substantive. Not only is something good, but the thing described becomes *a good* in itself, independently of reference to anything else. This language is remarkably similar to what has come to be known as the 'basic goods theory' of morality developed by a particular school of moral philosophers.[52] According to this theory, these 'goods' may never be damaged nor may they be compared with each other, as in an ethical conflict. "Basic goods" are thus inviolable, and the encyclical puts forth this theory to give substance to what it understands by the natural law.

> Precisely because of this "truth" *the natural law involves universality*. Inasmuch as it is inscribed in the rational nature of the person, it makes itself felt to all beings endowed with reason and living in history. In order to perfect himself in his specific order, the person must do good and avoid evil, be concerned for the transmission and preservation of life, refine and develop the riches of the material world, cultivate social life, seek truth, practice good and contemplate beauty. (*VS*, 51)

---

52. The primary practitioners of this theory are Germain G. Grisez, *The Way of the Lord Jesus*. Vol. 1: *Christian Moral Principles* (Chicago: Franciscan Herald Press, 1983), esp. Chapter 5, Quest. D, "The Goods which fulfill persons"; and John Finnis, *Moral Absolutes: Tradition, Revision and Truth* (Washington: C.U.A. Press, 1991). The basic goods theory tries to revive and to expand one interpretation of how Thomas attempted to explain the function of the natural law in *S.T.* I-II, q. 94, a. 2. Basically, to illustrate his point, after laying out his concept of the natural law being little more than the knowledge of the first principle of practical reasoning (good is to be done and pursued, and evil is to be avoided), Thomas suggests that we gain a glimpse into the 'content' of what might be 'good' (that to which all things are attracted) by considering our 'inclinations'. In typically logical fashion, using the classical definition of a person being a "rational animal", he lays out the things to which we are inclined as substances, as animals and as rational creatures. Thomas did not intend to create a hierarchy with his illustration, for it is more than obvious that the good as perceived through reason (to know the truth about God and to live in society) is a 'higher' good than that to which we are inclined as mere substances (self-preservation). Advocates of the 'basic goods theory' have expanded the 'list' of basic goods to seven or eight items, depending upon which publication one consults.

The modification of the classical text of Thomas (*S.T.*, I-II, q. 94, a. 2)[53] which is cited at this point in footnote 93 is evidence of the influence of the 'basic goods' school on the text of the encyclical. It represents a revival of natural law theory that signifies a step away from the teaching of Vatican II that replaced 'nature' with the *human person* as the focal point for determining good and evil and ultimately right and wrong.

What is good is good for the person, not (necessarily) what is good for the person's substantive, vegetative or animal nature. The texts of Vatican II, and a number of post-conciliar moral theologians, recognized that in order to discern what the good-for-the-person might be, it is inadequate to consult merely our 'inclinations' or 'typical behavior'. Contemporary psychology and sociology have taught us that what huge numbers of people consider to be 'natural inclinations' are nothing more than learned reflexes supported by a social-political-economic structure that has little to do with nature and a great deal to do with cultural history. Thus, many people believe that it is completely 'natural' (i.e., it is typical human behavior) to accumulate possessions beyond one's needs, to stratify society according to natural tendencies to lead and to follow, to destroy or at least to neutralize one's enemies, to allow 'market forces' to dictate our economic destiny, or simply to accept that white european male persons are endowed with characteristics that make them superior to non-white persons, non-european ethnic groups and non-male citizens. The latter may enjoy certain civil rights granted to them by the political establishments of the world, but they have no justifiable claim to shoulder the burdens of responsibility equally with their male counterparts in the ecclesial community because they suffer from *natural* differences that pre-determine their rightful 'place' in the Reign of God.

This is the 'basic goods theory' - when one looks below the surface. This is natural law revisionism. It is simple, compact, predictable, and internally consistent. Unfortunately, it does not respond to the experience of a growing number of people both inside and outside the church who

---

53. This list differs from that of Thomas by including, "... refine and develop the riches of the material world, ... practice good and contemplate beauty." It differs even more radically by claiming that what "... is inscribed in the *rational* nature of the person" (emphasis added) includes things like being "... concerned for the transmission and preservation of life." This particular good, according to Thomas, is typical of our *animal*, not our rational nature.

would follow another route for establishing the basis or focal point for determining what is good or evil, right or wrong.

In 1964-1965, as the "Pastoral Constitution on the Church in the Modern World," *Gaudium et Spes*, was taking its final shape, the text had already reached the stage of having two major parts: a statement of fundamental principles (Part I, 4 chapters), and an application of those principles to "problems of special urgency" (Part II, 5 chapters on marriage, culture, socio-economics, political life, and peace). The intervening paragraph between Parts I & II stated what procedure would be followed in the consideration of these problems. Bringing its own particular contribution to bear on issues facing the whole of humankind, one would expect the council to invoke the traditional Catholic sources of scripture, tradition and the natural law. Had it done so, moral theology would probably not have been revised and *Veritatis Splendor* would probably not have been written.

Gaudium et Spes did not and does not invoke natural law. It makes no appeal to our 'natural inclinations'. It has no theory of basic, fundamental, natural or absolute goods that can be spoken of apart from persons who are situated in a real human environment with all its complexity, conflict and challenge. To these situations and to the problems of special urgency to which the council turned its attention, the Pastoral Constitution offered its consideration "in the light of the gospel and of human experience" (*GS*, 46).

With this simple statement, the council altered the direction of concentration for the discipline of moral theology. No longer was it sufficient to isolate 'the good' that had to be protected and promoted at all costs. The ultimate criterion for 'good' itself had become the human person. No longer was it sufficient to begin with the 'object' of human action. Human experience demonstrated that a truly human act was always a motivated, circumstantial event that has meaning only in its entirety and in its context.

The shift from 'the good' to 'the person' as the central, first and fundamental focal point for moral analysis had a profound effect upon the rest of moral theology. As long as one begins with an abstract notion of 'the good' based upon a theory of human psychology that presumes all inclinations are 'natural inclinations' and that all natural inclinations *ipso facto* determine the content of moral good, one is trapped in a system that prioritizes goods over persons, and subsequently physical actions over human actions. It is not the endorsement of the priority of the *object* of the act (over the intention and circumstances) that determines the preference for 'the good' rather than 'the person', but exactly the opposite. If one chooses the priority of 'the good' which is absolute, non-contextual, non-historical and non-empirical (i.e., not based in human experience), one *must* endorse a moral analysis that places the *object* of physical action as the primary criterion for moral judgment. Goods come first, persons come second; and since the law (rule, norm, etc.) points to 'the good' or warns about damaging 'the good', the law becomes more important than persons, conscience, freedom or responsibility.

John Paul II has come to be known as a 'personalist' moral theologian who relies upon a phenomenological method for moral analysis. It therefore came as something of a surprise to find this latest encyclical endorsing a philosophical method that is not consistent with much of his earlier work, especially in the field of social ethics. At the same time, considering the complex, technical language utilized by the second chapter of that text, a language that would be more familiar to a theologian reading his or her way through the literature than to a pastor going to, meeting and listening to, praying with and praying for the people of God, one has to conclude to at least some degree of multiple authorship. At the same time, considering the fact that a great deal of contemporary - even pre-conciliar - moral theology has been occupied precisely with questions of conflict, choosing the greater good or lesser evil, and justifying the sacrifice of a good even if this occurs merely as an effect of one's action (principles of double effect, totality, and material cooperation), it appears as well that the theory put forth here is not in line with mainstream Roman Catholic moral theological tradition.

Some Remarks on the Use of Scripture in *Veritatis Splendor*

Gareth Moore

Scripture occupies an important place in the way *Veritatis Splendor* is presented. The intention of John Paul II in this encyclical is to deal with "certain fundamental questions regarding the Church's moral teaching" (*VS*, 5). The purpose of the encyclical is defined more precisely as

> to set forth, with regard to the problems being discussed, the principles of a moral teaching based upon Sacred Scripture and the living Apostolic Tradition, and at the same time to shed light on the presuppositions and consequences of the dissent which that teaching has met. (*ibid.*)

Here scripture and tradition are seen as the twin pillars on which the moral teaching of the church rests. But tradition, as the authentic interpretation of scripture, is logically secondary to scripture, and it becomes clear later in the encyclical that it is on scripture that the main weight is to be laid; scripture is *the* foundation of moral teaching. Thus at the beginning of chapter two, John Paul asserts that

> Sacred Scripture remains the living and fruitful source of the Church's moral doctrine; as the Second Vatican Council recalled, the Gospel is "the source of all saving truth and moral teaching". (*VS*, 28)

And he recalls how the Second Vatican Council

> invited scholars to take "special care for the renewal of moral theology", in such a way that "its scientific presentation, increasingly based on the teaching of Scripture, will cast light on the exalted vocation of the faithful in Christ and on their obligation to bear fruit in charity for the life of the world". (*VS*, 29)

Towards the end of the encyclical John Paul expresses the hope that, along
with the magisterium, moral theologians will be

> deeply concerned to clarify ever more fully the biblical found-
> ations, the ethical significance and the anthropological concerns
> which underlie the moral doctrine and the vision of man set forth
> by the Church. (*VS*, 110)

It is of course this great concern that moral teaching should be seen to be
based on scripture that underlies the long meditation on Matthew's version
of the story of the rich young man in chapter one. The purpose of this is
precisely to begin to show how scripture provides the basis of morality.
In view of this scriptural emphasis it is also not surprising that the
encyclical abounds in scriptural citations, references and allusions.[1] The
many subsections of the three chapters have their own heading, and only
a dozen or so of these (concentrated in chapter 3) fail to cite or refer to
a scriptural passage.

It would be a long task, and would perhaps be to little purpose, to examine
every one of the references to scripture contained in the encyclical. Some
of these are more central than others, their accuracy more or less crucial
to the argument. In a work of such length mistakes are bound to creep in;
some of these are of little consequence, and they will not be mentioned.
I intend, rather, to concentrate on the encyclical's treatment of a very few
scriptural passages, to see whether the pope fulfills his ambition in that
treatment, whether he does manage to establish a biblical basis for morality
in the desired sense. Following an order suggested by the encyclical itself,
I shall first survey the treatment of the story of the rich young man which
occupies such a large part of chapter one; my discussion of this and its
ramifications will constitute the bulk of what I have to say. I shall end by
examining briefly the role of scripture in the argumentation of chapter two.
This heavy emphasis on chapter one and on the story of the rich young man
will, I hope, be justified by the diversity and importance of the issues the
encyclical's treatment of Mt 19:16-30 raises; some of these are also
relevant to the argument of chapter two. I cannot deny that such a bias
entails omitting any discussion of several important points raised by other

---

1. At the end of this contribution is included a summary of explicit citations and references
to the different books of the Old and New Testaments.

aspects of the encyclical's treatment of scripture. I have the consolation that my words will receive nothing like the attention afforded the pope's.

The Rich Young Man

I have referred above to the treatment of the story of the rich young man as a meditation because that is how the pope himself describes it (*VS*, 28). I think few could fail to be impressed with it considered as a meditation. The lessons for believers which the pope draws from this passage of Matthew are deep and important. For the young man, John Paul tells us, the question "What good must I do to have eternal life?" is not so much about rules to be followed, but about the "full meaning of life". It is "ultimately an appeal to the absolute Good which attracts us and beckons us; it is the echo of a call from God who is the origin and goal of man's life" (*VS*, 7). It is our ultimate purpose to live for the glory of God (*VS*, 10). The fulfillment of the Law can come only as a gift of God, "the offer of a share in the divine Goodness revealed and communicated in Jesus" (*VS*, 11). "Love of neighbor springs from a loving heart which, precisely because it loves, is ready to live out the loftiest challenges" (*VS*, 15). "The follower of Christ knows that his vocation is to freedom" (*VS*, 17). And so on.

Without questioning the importance of such lessons, it is legitimate to ask whether they are really what is taught in this encounter of Jesus with the rich young man. For if scripture is to be the basis of moral teaching, this must mean more than that passages like Mt 19:16-30 present an occasion for weaving a meditation that presents moral truths which are independently believed. Those truths must be in some way contained in the meaning of the scriptural passage itself. The effort to discover the meaning of a text demands that the text be approached in a manner which is open to receiving what it actually says. This means resisting as far as possible any temptation to read cherished beliefs into it, or to think that *this* is what the text *must* mean. A successful and convincing *exegesis* entails eschewing *eisegesis*. Only in this way is the project of finding a biblical basis for Catholic moral teaching, which the pope, following the Second Vatican Council, considers so important, furthered. The question arises, therefore, does this moving meditation on the story of the rich young man also represent a successful exegesis of the passage? Doubts can be raised about this on a number of points, and I will now explore some of these.

John Paul claims that

> in the young man, whom Matthew's Gospel does not name, we can
> recognize every person who, consciously or not, approaches Christ
> the Redeemer of man and questions him about morality. (*VS*, 7)

While it is true to say that gospel stories often make more than one point,
this initial approach to this story obscures what, from the content and
context of the story in the gospel itself, is the narrative's main point, which
is that the encounter provides an example of the power of riches over those
who own them and an occasion for the teaching of Jesus on how hard it
is for the rich to enter the kingdom of heaven (19:23ff). In all three
synoptic gospels the encounter and the teaching are linked; indeed in Luke
the teaching is delivered as part of the encounter and is addressed to the
ruler (not a young man in Luke, nor is he young in Mark). To emphasize
the link between the encounter and the teaching, and also to heighten the
dramatic effect of the story, the information that the man is rich is withheld
to the end (or near the end in Luke's case) of the meeting. We do not know
where the story is leading until he becomes sorrowful (in Matthew and
Mark he goes away sorrowful) and we learn the reason for his sorrow.
Understood in this way the story also provides a complement to the incident
of the young children (Mt 19:13-15; cf. Mk 10:13-16; Lk 18:15-17) which
it immediately follows. It is to such as these children that the kingdom of
heaven belongs (19:14); for the rich, on the other hand, of whom our
young man is a virtuous example, it will be extremely difficult to enter the
kingdom of heaven (19:23). Thus "many that are first will be last, and the
last first" (19:30).

The encyclical all but ignores this central meaning of the passage. It is
noted that the young man went away sorrowful (*VS*, 22), but the fact that
he is rich and the following teaching on the dangers of riches, with its vivid
language designed to catch the attention ("a camel through the eye of a
needle") are passed over in silence in favor of an emphasis on Jesus's
remark that with God all things are possible (19:26), which leads to an
extended section on grace (*VS*, 22-24). Jesus's teaching on the power of
God is of course important, but so is his teaching on riches, and it is to
distort the meaning of this passage to treat it as being about the commandments and grace at the cost of ignoring what it has to say about riches.

I suspect one reason why John Paul does this is his determination to find a universal message in this story: as we see from the quotation from the encyclical above, the man represents *everybody* who asks Jesus about morality; and Jesus's encouragement to him to sell all his goods and give the money to the poor is meant for *everyone* (*VS*, 18). To give weight to the fact that here Jesus is addressing a *rich* man detracts from the potential universality of application of Jesus's teaching in this passage. However, why should we believe that what Jesus says in a particular context to a specific person *must* be of universal import, must apply to everybody? In this particular case the exhortation to give all to the poor surely is not meant to apply to the poor. The gospels show Jesus giving instruction to and about a number of different types of person - the rich, the poor, the disciples, the crowd, hypocrites, the self-righteous, the powerful, the helpless, religious leaders, *etc*. In the typical case, the people concerned, if they are individuals appearing in the narrative, are anonymous. (John Paul rightly notes this of the rich young man.) This gives them the status of the typical; what Jesus says of them is universal in that it applies to everybody of their type. But much of the power of Jesus's words comes from the fact that he does not only talk in generalities but addresses people with *specific* characteristics, faults and problems. To rob his words of their specificity by finding a universal message in everything he says is to risk robbing them of their power.

The encyclical makes much of the fact that Jesus replies to the man by referring to the commandments:

> Jesus tells the young man: "If you wish to enter into life, keep the commandments" (Mt 19:17). In this way, a close connection is made between eternal life and obedience to God's commandments: God's commandments show man the path of life and they lead to it. From the very lips of Jesus, the new Moses, man is once again given the commandments of the Decalogue. Jesus himself definitively confirms them and proposes them to us as the way and condition of salvation. (*VS*, 12)

Thus the lesson to be drawn from this passage of the gospel is a very general one in its application. The implication is that the connection between eternal life and keeping the commandments is valid for everybody. Because the rich young man represents everybody, God's commandments' show, not this rich young man, but *everybody* the path of life. Note too how from this comment about the commandments in general the focus is narrowed down rapidly to the decalogue. Later on this will be developed in the direction of the universal necessity to keep especially the negative precepts of the law. This may be a sound doctrine, but it is doubtful for a number of reasons whether it can be drawn from this passage of Matthew's gospel.

To begin with, though 'eternal life' is not a common phrase in the synoptic gospels, this is not the only place in Matthew where eternal life is spoken of. It occurs also in the parable of the sheep and the goats (25:31-46). The accursed goats will go away into eternal punishment, but the righteous sheep into eternal life (v. 46).[2] This parable is particularly significant in Matthew's gospel, as it represents the final words of Jesus's teaching ministry; after this the gospel moves into the narrative of the passion. The words 'eternal life' are also in a very emphatic position, at the very end of the parable. Further, this parable is not addressed to a particular person in a particular situation, but appears to be general teaching. If anything, then, we might expect this parable, rather than the story of the rich young man, to provide the most significant indication of Jesus's teaching on what is needed to enter eternal life. If we ask what are the conditions said here to be necessary, they are elementary works of mercy: feeding the hungry, welcoming the stranger, clothing the naked, visiting the sick and imprisoned. These works may be regarded as ways of fulfilling the general command to love one's neighbor, though the connection is not made. None of the works mentioned here is commanded in the decalogue. The language of law is quite absent from this parable. In particular, there is no reference to the negative commandments which feature so largely later in the encyclical; the wicked are condemned not because they have infringed negative commandments, but because they have omitted to perform elementary acts of kindness.

It is in keeping with the attempt to derive a universal message from the story of the rich young man, one moreover in conformity with the project of founding morality on commandment, that there is no consideration given

---

2. The phrase 'eternal life' occurs in Mark only in his parallel to the story of the rich young man and its sequel (10:17,30); in Luke it occurs in his parallel to the same story (18:18,30), and also in 10:25. See below for a discussion of this passage.

to the function of Jesus's reply to this specific person in this particular narrative. But such a consideration is essential to an understanding of the dynamic of the encounter between Jesus and the young man. The young man is presented as an observant Jew, but not observant in the manner of the hypocritical Pharisees who sometimes make their appearance in the gospels. He does not have to be told to keep the commandments, as his reply to Jesus's reference to the decalogue and the command to love one's neighbor - a reply which Jesus accepts - makes clear. The dialogue between Jesus and the young man serves to bring this out, to stress his genuine goodness. He is not a sinner who needs to be corrected, or a hypocrite to be exposed, but one near perfection.[3] It may fairly be said that nobody else whom Jesus encounters in the course of his ministry is cast in such a favorable light. He is the only person in the synoptic gospels who initiates an encounter with Jesus and whom Jesus then asks to follow him. All of this serves to make the end of the encounter all the more poignant. Despite his good qualities he is unable to free himself from his wealth; and he knows his own failure, since he goes away *sorrowful*. This departure (marking the only failed call to discipleship in the gospels) provides the motive for the teaching on riches and entry into the kingdom which follows and which is integrally linked with it. The dialogue concerning the commandments (vv. 17-20) therefore serves a dramatic function, both building up a favorable picture of the young man and holding back the final disappointment, thereby making it more effective when it comes. That vv. 17-20 serve a dramatic rather than a didactic function is confirmed by the fact that neither the decalogue nor any other commandments are mentioned in the course of the instruction to the disciples. The message of this narrative is not how hard it is for those who do not keep the commandments to enter the kingdom, but how hard for those with riches.

In this connection it is instructive to note that Luke, who also recounts this incident, narrates another in which this very same question is asked, this time by a lawyer (Lk 10:25ff.). The reply given by Jesus to this same question, but put by a different person, is quite different. First, though as

---

3. The Markan version of the story emphasizes this more than the Matthean. When the man replies that he has kept all the commandments, Mark tells us that "Jesus, looking upon him, loved him"; and his encouragement to sell all and give to the poor is prefaced by "You lack one thing" (10:21; Luke has something very similar, Lk 18:22). Here the obvious import is that he lacks *only* one thing.

in the case of the rich young man he directs the lawyer's attention to the law, he invites the lawyer himself to pick out what he considers it contains necessary to eternal life. The lawyer does not pick out one or more of the commandments of the decalogue, but replies: "You shall love the Lord your God with all your heart, and with all your soul, and with all your strength, and with all your mind: and your neighbor as yourself", conflating the commandment of Deuteronomy 6:4 and that of Leviticus 19:18.[4] This answer Jesus confirms as correct and adds: "Do this, and you will live". He does not feel the need to supplement this with any reference to any other commandments, from either the decalogue or elsewhere. He leaves it up to the lawyer to work out for himself what this love of God and love of neighbor implies. In this case Jesus does not consider it necessary to introduce other - negative - commandments, as he does with the rich young man. This confirms again that the reference to these commandments of the decalogue in that narrative has a purpose: it is designed to enable the young man to be shown as a good, law-abiding Jew, so that the conversation can be moved on in the direction of Jesus's call to discipleship.

This is not the point of the Lucan narrative. Hence neither does Jesus in Luke invite the lawyer to sell all he has, give to the poor and follow him. Rather does the encounter move on to Jesus's parable of the Good Samaritan, picking up the second half of the lawyer's reply and shedding light on what it is to be a neighbor. This confirms that the call to the rich young man to sell and give to the poor is not to be interpreted as meant for everybody, but is connected with the point of the story as Matthew (in agreement with Mark and Luke) presents it, namely the danger of riches. Here in Luke the story of the lawyer is told for a different purpose, and so proceeds in another direction.

I wish now to look in more detail at the second part of this story from Matthew, the dialogue with the disciples, and at how it is treated by the encyclical. As I stated above, this dialogue makes it clear that the main point of the narrative of the encounter with the rich young man is to lead to Jesus's teaching on the relation between riches and the kingdom of

---

4. In Matthew (22:34-40) and Mark (12:28-34) Jesus is shown citing these two commandments himself, in answer to the questions "Which is the greatest commandment of the law?" and "Which commandment is the first of all?" respectively.

heaven. At the end of the encounter the man goes away sorrowful "for he had great possessions" (19:22), and Jesus immediately initiates the dialogue with the disciples by declaring: "Truly, I say to you, it will be hard for a rich man to enter the kingdom of heaven" (19:23). The encyclical, however, passes over these words of Jesus in silence. It mentions only the disciples' reaction:

> Not only the rich man but the disciples themselves are taken aback by Jesus' call to discipleship, the demands of which transcend human aspirations and abilities: "When the disciples heard this, they were greatly astounded and said, 'Then who can be saved?'" (Mt 19:25).

The disciples, we are told, are astonished by Jesus's call of the rich young man to discipleship. But they are not. If they were, their reaction would be very strange. Why should they express their astonishment at Jesus calling somebody to discipleship by exclaiming "Who then can be saved"? Their astonishment is not at the fact that Jesus called the young man to follow him, nor at the man's departure in sorrow. They are bewildered by Jesus's words to them, the words which the encyclical entirely omits to treat here or, as far as I can tell, at any point. The reaction of the disciples appears to reflect the belief, common in the Old Testament, that riches, when the possession of the pious, are God's blessing and a sign of his favor (see, e.g., Job 1:1-3,10; 42:7-17; Ps 128(127); 1 Kgs 3:10-13; Deut 28:1-14). Salvation is a matter of God's favor; if one so favored by God, like the rich young man, cannot be saved, then it seems that nobody can.

This is the context in which Jesus says: "With men this is impossible, but with God all things are possible" (Mt 19:26). For the encyclical these words are an affirmation that divine grace is necessary if one is to live as a disciple. "To imitate and live out the love of Christ is not possible for man by his own strength alone. He becomes capable of this love only by virtue of a gift received" (VS, 22). From this we move on to Paul's words in Romans 8:2 "The law of the Spirit of life in Christ Jesus has set me free from the law of sin and death" (VS, 23). The disciple, then, receives new life, and "Only in this new life is it possible to carry out God's commandments. Indeed, it is through faith in Christ that we have been made righteous (cf. Rom 3:28): the righteousness which the Law demands, but is unable to give, is found by every believer to be revealed and granted by the Lord Jesus" (ibid.).

Morality and Law

However, this line of thought takes as its starting point an interpretation of 19:26 which is, as we have seen, erroneous. Further, for Jesus, in this part of Matthew's gospel, being saved cannot be equivalent to being given the grace to make it possible to carry out God's commandments, as the encyclical asserts. Jesus has already made it clear, in his conversation with the young man and in response to his request for clarification ("Which?" 19:18), what is to be understood as the commandments of God as far as this passage is concerned; they are the commandments of the Old Testament law. And these the young man has already been able to keep. In 19:26 Jesus cannot, therefore, if he has in mind something the young man lacks, be referring to the ability to obey the commandments. His words seem to point, rather, to the necessity of something apart from obedience to law, to the inadequacy of thinking of a person's relationship to God in terms of law and commandment.

If for Jesus in Mt 19:26 grace is not accurately spoken of as the grace which gives us the ability to obey the commandments, neither is it true that Paul thinks of the life of the Spirit, the life of faith, as that in which we are made able to obey the commandments of God, as the encyclical seems to imply. Paul's language is complex, but he nowhere says or implies that the Spirit is given us that we might be obedient. The Spirit is indeed the source of good works, but the Christian does not perform those works as one subject to law (Gal 5:16-23). He holds that people are justified by faith "apart from works of law" (Rom 3:28; Phil 3:4-11). Grace is the free gift of life not based on works of the law (Rom 4:13-16). Thus for Paul, too, a person's relationship to God is not properly thought of in terms of obedience to commandment, even obedience made possible by the Spirit.

This point, as well as the mention above of Luke's account of the meeting with the lawyer and of the parable of the sheep and the goats, brings to our attention a wider question. Any attempt to found morality on scripture is faced with the problem where to start. There is a lot of scripture; some parts contradict others and some parts have traditionally been regarded as more central than others. One has inevitably to be selective, but one's selection also has to be justified. I have already given reasons for saying that the story of the rich young man is not a good place to start - at least if one wishes to go in the direction the encyclical takes - because of reasons internal to the story itself; the use the encyclical makes of it distorts it in a number of ways. But we must now also ask: why should one want to start here at all? Why not with the parable of the sheep and the goats, or with Luke's story of the meeting with the lawyer? We might accept that we should begin by looking to the actions and words of Jesus, since we are his disciples; but if the story of the rich young man "can serve as a useful guide for listening once more in a lively and direct way to his moral teaching" (*VS*, 6), so can the parable of the sheep and the goats and the story of the meeting with the lawyer. If "in her reflection on morality, the Church has always kept in mind the words of Jesus to the rich young man" (*VS*, 28), it has also always kept in mind Matthew 25 and Luke 10, and many other words and actions of Jesus besides. Some of these have a rather wider message than the narrative of Matthew 19, and might be expected to provide a wider and more solid biblical support for Christian morality.

The choice of the story of the rich young man appears motivated by a desire not simply to listen to what Jesus says, but to stress one particular mode of biblical discourse among several, namely the legal. The desire to speak of morality in terms of law, of commandments and obedience to them, is evident throughout the encyclical.[5] The encounter with the rich young man appears to be suitable for this purpose, since in it Jesus enjoins the young man to keep the commandments, and the encyclical's treatment of this encounter, as well as of the following dialogue with the disciples, is centered around this injunction. I have tried to show that this approach distorts the natural sense of this passage, but nevertheless in the context of the encyclical this treatment is important as it prepares the way for the

---

5. A brief indication of the importance of legal terminology in the encyclical is afforded by the section headings. Thus chapter two contains sections headed "Blessed is the man who takes delight in the law of the Lord (cf. Ps 1:1-2)" (*VS*, 42-45) and "What the law requires is written on their hearts (Rom 2:15)" (*VS*, 46-50). In chapter three we find "Martyrdom, the exaltation of the inviolable holiness of God's law" (*VS*, 90-94) and "Grace and obedience to God's law" (*VS*, 102-105). From among the many occurrences in the text itself (the word "law" occurs over 230 times in the English translation, "commandment" some 126 times), the following may suffice as examples. The Sermon on the Mount "contains the fullest and most complete formulation of the New Law" (*VS*, 12). Jesus is "a living and personal Law" (*VS*, 15). Human freedom "is called to accept the moral law given by God. In fact, human freedom finds its authentic and complete fulfillment precisely in the acceptance of that law" (*VS*, 35). The church teaches that the "natural moral law has God as its author" (*VS*, 36). "Law must therefore be considered an expression of divine wisdom: by submitting to the law, freedom submits to the truth of creation" (*VS*, 41).

great emphasis on morality as obedience to law, made possible by grace, which pervades the rest of the encyclical.

The legal material is of course there in the bible to be used. There is no doubt that it forms a significant aspect of biblical thought, and this must not be forgotten. However, the attitude displayed to law in the New Testament is not uniform, and in an encyclical which emphasizes scripture and law so much, the failure to deal with this fact produces an unbalanced impression and cannot but be seen as a defect. The synoptic gospel upon which the encyclical draws most freely is Matthew's. I counted 68 references to Matthew, and only 12 from Mark and 20 from Luke; although 29 of the references to Matthew are to verses within the range 19:16-30, even if these are ignored there are still more references to Matthew than to Mark and Luke together. As is widely recognized, Matthew's is the most consistently Jewish of the synoptic gospels in flavor. And obedience to the law was central to Jewish piety. It is no surprise, then, that Matthew's gospel is the most favored in the encyclical. But some attention is owed to the fact that Mark and Luke, writing for audiences and from a background different from Matthew's, are less concerned with the provisions of the law, and less concerned to think in legal terms.

For example, the radicalization of the demands of the law found in Mt 5:21-48 is not to be found in Luke. Some of the material is to be found at various points in Luke's gospel, but it is not cast in terms of an interpretation of the law. For example, Mt 5:44 "But I say to you, Love your enemies and pray for those who persecute you" has a parallel in Lk 6:27 "Love your enemies, do good to those who hate you"; but in Luke this teaching is not presented, as it is in Matthew, as a comment on the commandment to love one's neighbor (glossed with "and hate your enemy") found in Lev 19:18 (cf. Mt 5:43). Again, in both Matthew and Luke, Jesus criticizes the scribes and Pharisees for assiduously tithing herbs while neglecting weightier matters (Mt 23:23; Lk 11:42; the weightier matters are justice, mercy and faith in Matthew, and justice and the love of God in Luke). But in Matthew these are referred to as weightier matters *of the law*, and this phrase is absent from the Lucan parallel. These differences do not mean that the references to law in Matthew are unimportant, but they do suggest that the evangelists are concerned to couch the message of Jesus in language suitable to their audiences.

Even within Matthew's gospel the approach to law is not uniform. Although Jesus says that not a jot or a tittle will pass away, he justifies the actions of his disciples when they are accused of violating the sabbath law by plucking ears of grain (12:1-8). Interestingly, he does so not by denying that they are doing anything unlawful, but by pointing to other instances of violation of the law - the consumption of the bread of the presence by David and his followers (12:3f) and the profanation of the sabbath by the temple priests (12:5).

Further variety is provided by John. In John's gospel Jesus appears to be deliberately distanced from the law of Moses. In the prologue it is stated that "the law was given through Moses; grace and truth came through Jesus Christ" (1:17); a contrast seems implied, though it is not spelt out precisely what this contrast is. When speaking to the Jews Jesus refers to the law as "your law" (8:17; 10:34); the evangelist speaks of "their law" (15:25). Jesus speaks to the disciples of his commandments, which the disciples will keep if they love him (14:15,21; 15:10). But when it comes to spelling these out Jesus speaks only of a single commandment, the commandment to love another as he has loved them (13:34; 15:12). There is no concern to expound and deepen the law of Moses such as is found in the Sermon on the Mount, and no reference to negative precepts of the kind found in the story of the rich young man.

These considerations make it questionable whether an approach to the moral teaching of Jesus in terms of law and commandment should be given the privileged status it enjoys in the encyclical. The encyclical's claim to be presenting the biblical foundations of morality are seriously compromised if its scriptural focus is narrowed to one type of discourse, which is emphasized much more in some parts of scripture than in others, and to which there is by no means a uniform scriptural attitude.

Morality and Holiness

There are other difficulties, connected with exegesis, which lie in the way of founding morality initially on the commandments of the decalogue, however this approach may be modified and developed by stressing Christ as the fulfillment of the law and human dependence on grace. The decalogue makes its first appearance in *VS*, 10, in this way:

> In the "ten words" of the Covenant with Israel, and in the whole Law, God makes himself known and acknowledged as the One

who alone is good; the One who despite man's sin remains the
model for moral action, in accordance with his command, "You
shall be holy; for I the Lord your God am holy" (Lev 19:2).

It is clear that for this encyclical the decalogue is not to be considered in
isolation from "the whole law"; if emphasis is laid on the decalogue, indeed
on parts of it, this must not be allowed to obscure the fact that there is a
great deal more to the law than the ten commandments. In connection with
this, it is not quite correct to say that the decalogue constitutes the terms
of the covenant. In the covenant ratification ceremony of Ex 24:3-8, in
which Moses writes "all the words of the Lord" (24:4) and reads them to
the people, who agree to do "all that the Lord has spoken" (24:7), it is
clear that the words referred to are not just the decalogue but the
succeeding legislation contained in chapters 21-23. Again, in Deuteronomy,
where the covenant theme is more developed, the "words of the covenant"
(29:1; heb 28:69) are the not only the decalogue (5:6-21) but the whole of
the law of Deuteronomy.

However, a problem immediately arises in such an attempt to found
morality in the first instance on the commandments of the Old Testament
law, even if one then wishes to go on to link this to the law of love and
invoke grace as the means by which obedience is made possible. By no
means are all the laws those which we would recognize as moral. There
are, for example, many cultic and agricultural laws which appear to us to
have no moral import. In order, perhaps, to surmount this problem and
begin to lay the foundations of morality on a biblical view of law, this
passage of the encyclical makes a connection between morality and the
command "You shall be holy, for I the Lord your God am holy",
interpreting the whole law as a call to holiness. It is a summons to imitate
God, "the model for moral action". Thus the encyclical sees a single moral
demand underlying the whole law, even, presumably, the apparently non-
moral laws. As revelation progresses, the true imitation of God will be
revealed as the imitation of Christ.

Jesus himself is the living 'fulfillment' of the Law inasmuch as
he fulfills its authentic meaning by the total gift of himself: he
himself becomes a living and personal Law, who invites people

to follow him. (*VS*, 15)[6]

However, the call to be holy as it appears in Leviticus is not a moral exhortation, as John Paul presents it. In the Old Testament holiness is not a moral concept. The part of Leviticus in which this commandment is to be found (the "Holiness Code") does indeed contain commandments which we would think of as moral, such as "You shall not oppress you neighbor or rob him" (19:13) and "You shall do no injustice in judgment" (19:15); but it also contains the commandments "You shall not sow your field with two kinds of seed; nor shall there come upon you a garment of cloth made of two kinds of stuff" (19:19) and "You shall not eat any flesh with the blood in it" (19:26). Lying with a male as with a woman may be an abomination (18:22), but so is eating the flesh of a peace offering on the third day after the sacrifice (19:7). While we might regard the former as concerned with moral behavior, the latter does not speak to our moral concerns. The laws of these chapters cut across our categories of the moral and non-moral; they are not concerned with morality. The holiness of the Israelites is rather a matter of their separation to God and from the surrounding peoples and their ways. Thus we find also "You shall be holy to me; for I the Lord am holy, and have separated you from the peoples, that you should be mine" (20:26).

This is the explanation of why, though in Leviticus the call to become holy is important, in Deuteronomy, where there is an equal stress on holiness, there is no *call* to holiness. The holiness of the people is taken as an established fact, since God has chosen Israel, separating it from the nations. In Deuteronomy the refrain is not "You shall be holy" but "You *are* holy" (see *e.g.* 7:6; 14:2,21). Deuteronomy does not mean by this that the people of Israel lead a moral life; on the contrary, it is concerned to portray them in an unfavorable light (see *e.g.* 9:4-29).

Selecting Commandments

In so far as the commandments, epitomized by the decalogue, are concerned with holiness, they do not obviously furnish a foundation for the

---

6. Cf. "The way and at the same time the content of this perfection consist in the following of Jesus" (*VS*, 19); "Jesus asks us to follow him and to imitate him along the path of love" (*VS*, 20).

moral life. Many of them of course speak to our moral concerns, but many do not. In *VS*, 25 the encyclical speaks of the Old Testament law as "the moral prescriptions which God imparted in the Old Covenant" which "must be faithfully kept and continually put into practice in the various different cultures throughout the course of history."[7] This is a misleading description if it is meant to designate the overall purpose of the Old Testament law, or if it is meant to apply to all of its prescriptions. It may be that only a selection of the laws is intended to serve as a foundation for morality, but then the criteria for selection have to be stated and justified. The underlying assumption may be that it is only those laws which appear to us as moral (rather than, say, cultic) which are important for Christian moral teaching and which we are required to keep; and this would surely be a reasonable assumption. But it is not itself biblical. The Old Testament law itself contains no criteria by which it may be determined which of its provisions may be set aside; *all* of it must be kept, as is recognized by Paul (see Gal 5:3) and James (2:10). Susanna is commended in the encyclical as a martyr, willing to face death rather than commit adultery, forbidden by the law (*VS*, 91); but Eleazar, along with seven brothers and their mother, was equally willing to die a martyr's death rather than break the commandment not to eat pork (2 Macc 6:18-7:41). There is no distinction between the moral and the cultic laws operative here. Neither is one established in the New Testament. Jesus declares that not a jot or tittle of the law will pass away, making no distinction between moral laws and others (Mt 5:18). Twice Jesus tells those he has cured of leprosy to fulfil the cultic requirements of the Mosaic law with regard to their cleansing (Mt 8:1-4; Lk 17:11-19); and of course he observes the feasts prescribed by the law. The Council of Jerusalem urges disciples to refrain from unchastity, but also from eating blood (Acts 15:29).

If, as seems to be the case, the encyclical does nevertheless wish to make a distinction between moral commandments and others, in order to say that the former are binding and the latter not, we need to ask what is the criterion for distinguishing the two. In many cases the distinction may be clear to us: the commandment against murder is clearly moral in our terms, while the prescription that a bird be killed over running water for the cleansing of a leper (Lev 14:6) is equally clearly not. But many other cases

---

7. It also speaks of "the morality of the commandments" (*VS*, 11) and "the young man's commitment to respect all the moral demands of the commandments" (*VS*, 17).

are not so clear: Is the law forbidding people to wear clothes made of two
kinds of stuff (Lev 20:19) to be regarded as a moral law? Or the law
forbidding men and women to wear clothes associated with the other sex
(Deut 22:5)? The prohibition on a man's having sexual intercourse with
a menstruating woman (Lev 18:19), or with another man (Lev 18:22)? Is
the sabbath commandment moral, or ritual? It is impossible to settle such
questions by reference to the concerns of the human authors of the law in
question, since we often have no detailed idea what their intentions were,
and where we can form a general idea, as with the holiness code of
Leviticus, the scriptural concern appears to cut across our distinction
between the moral and the non-moral.

There is scriptural help to hand at this point. The Levitical commandment
"You shall love your neighbor as yourself" has great importance in the
New Testament. It is referred to and given fundamental significance some
seven times in the synoptic gospels, Paul and James.[8] It is thus in keeping
with the biblical aspirations of the encyclical that it places great emphasis
on this law at a number of points. Thus, for example, we find in the
meditation on the story of the rich young man:

> ... we cannot fail to notice which commandments of the Law the
> Lord recalls to the young man. They are some of the
> commandments belonging to the so-called second tablet of the
> Decalogue, the summary (cf. Rom 13:8-10) and foundation of
> which is the commandment of love of neighbor: "You shall love
> your neighbor as yourself". (VS, 13)

The commandments are said to "represent the basic condition for love of
neighbor; at the same time they are the proof of that love" (VS, 13). Following
a reference to Jesus's words that on the commandment to love God and the
commandment to love one's neighbor "depend all the Law and the Prophets"
(Mt 22:40), John Paul asserts that "Both the Old and the New Testaments
explicitly affirm that without love of neighbor, made concrete in keeping the
commandments, genuine love for God is not possible" (VS, 14). Jesus, he
affirms, "brings God's commandments to fulfillment, particularly the
commandment of love of neighbor, by interiorizing their demands and by
bringing out their fullest meaning" (VS, 15). And so on.

---

8. Mt 19:19; 22:39; Mk 12:31; Lk 10:27f; Rom 13:8-10; Gal 5:14; Jas 2:8.

Reference to the New Testament doctrine of love of neighbor as
fundamental to human living may be seen as providing a criterion for
deciding which of the commandments of the Old Testament law may be
regarded as moral, and although this is not stated explicitly it does seem
to underlie some of the encyclical's assertions. If it is true that "the
commandments" are the basic condition for love of neighbor (*VS*, 13),
there must surely be some implicit restriction on what commandments are
being referred to. Not wearing clothes made of two kinds of stuff cannot
plausibly be represented as a basic condition for love of neighbor, and
nowhere does John Paul attempt to show that any such law must be kept.

But if the commandment to love one's neighbor is being adopted as such a
criterion, this commandment cannot also be seen as simply a summary of the
law, as *VS*, 13 suggests,[9] since this leaves it unclear just what laws it is
supposed to be a summary of. In the course of chapter two of the encyclical,
which is concerned to show, among other things, that there are certain negative
commandments which may not be violated, it is asserted that

> When the Apostle Paul sums up the fulfillment of the law in the
> precept of love of neighbor as oneself (cf. Rom 13:8-10), he is
> not weakening the commandments but reinforcing them, since he
> is revealing their requirements and their gravity. Love of God and
> of one's neighbor cannot be separated from the observance of the
> commandments of the Covenant renewed in the blood of Jesus
> Christ and in the gift of the Spirit. (*VS*, 76)

Once again here we find "the commandments", and once again there must
be some kind of limitation on what commandments are being referred to.
That limitation must be supplied by the commandment to love itself. Some
commandments *are* weakened by Paul's statement in Rom 13:8-10, namely
those which have no relevance to love of neighbor. Again, discussing Gal
5:13f, the encyclical asserts that

---

9. See also *VS*, 76, quoted below, and *VS*, 83: "In him, who is the Truth (cf. Jn 14:6), man
can understand fully and live perfectly, through his good actions, his vocation to freedom in
obedience to the divine law summarized in the commandment of love of God and neighbor."
It has to be said that the language of "summary" is taken from Paul himself. He says in Rom
13:9 that the law is "summed up" (*anakephalaioutai*) in the commandment to love one's
neighbor. However, it will become clear that Paul's actual use of the love commandment is
as a criterion rather than as a mere summary.

> The firmness with which the Apostle opposes those who believe
> that they are justified by the Law has nothing to do with man's
> liberation from precepts. On the contrary, the latter are at the
> service of the practice of love: "For he who loves his neighbor
> has fulfilled the Law..." (*VS*, 17)

But there is a liberation from *some* precepts; this is the point of much of
what Paul says in Galatians. Those precepts remain which are necessary
for love of neighbor. But the accent is very much on love of neighbor, and
not on the fulfillment of precepts. Paul says "One who loves has fulfilled
the law"; not "One who loves will be careful to fulfil the precepts of the
law". Because love of neighbor is now seen as fundamental, the precepts
of the law are no longer to be obeyed simply because they are precepts.

This seems to me to have important consequences for the argument of the
encyclical as a whole, in so far as it claims to have a biblical basis. The
operative question is now not "What is prescribed or prohibited by the
law?" but "What does love of neighbor demand or allow?" Of course many
of the commandments of the law will be of help here, but many will not.
Plainly the commandments of the decalogue which Jesus mentions in the
encounter with the rich young man are important here. But how does this
relate to one of the central ideas of the encyclical, that there are negative
precepts which may never be violated? In the light of the above argument
it cannot be maintained that their inviolability derives simply from their
being precepts of the law. If the actions forbidden by these precepts may
never for any reason be performed, that must be because they can never,
in any circumstances, be compatible with love of neighbor. This is indeed
the position of the encyclical; the behavior forbidden by the negative
precepts is always wrong because "the choice of this kind of behavior is
in no case compatible with the goodness of the will of the acting person,
with his vocation to life with God and to communion with his neighbor"
(*VS*, 52). But this additional premise, though it may be true, is not itself
biblical. This places an important limitation on the biblical basis of
morality, precisely on the point which is for the encyclical one of the most
essential elements of Christian morality.

Morality and the Decalogue

If there are these general problems which emerge from the encyclical's treatment of Jesus's reference to law in the story of the rich young man, there are difficulties, too, attending its use of the particular laws of the decalogue that Jesus mentions. They, like the call to holiness, are interpreted as moral, serving to protect human goods. They

> are meant to safeguard *the good* of the person, the image of God, by protecting his *goods*. "You shall not murder; You shall not commit adultery; You shall not steal; You shall not bear false witness" are moral rules formulated in terms of prohibitions. These negative precepts express with particular force the ever urgent need to protect human life, the communion of persons in marriage, private property, truthfulness and people's good name. (*VS*, 13)

These words express a long-standing Christian understanding of these laws. However, in the Old Testament context their scope is rather narrower than this passage suggests. First, the law against murder does not reflect a recognition of the need to protect human life in general. The Hebrew verb translated "murder" denotes the premeditated malicious killing of one member of Israelite society by another. Some such law is necessary for the functioning of any society. There is no need to suppose that a desire to respect human life in general lies behind it. Indeed, the contrary is suggested by the law of war, in which it is commanded that all the males of a conquered city, if they try to resist conquest, be put to death (Deut 20:13), as well as the many laws for whose infraction the death penalty is prescribed (*e.g.*, adultery, Lev 20:10; incest, Lev 20:11f; wizardry, Lev 20:27; striking a parent, Ex 21:15; gathering sticks on the sabbath, Num 15:32-36).

Second, the law against adultery does not protect the communion of persons in marriage. It is designed rather to protect the sexual rights of husbands over their wives, rights which are akin to property rights. Hence the tenth commandment in the Exodus version of the decalogue ranks a neighbor's wife along with his house, his ox and "anything that is your neighbor's" (Ex 20:17). Hence also the absence of any law forbidding an Israelite woman from coveting her neighbor's husband. The woman next door does not have her rights infringed if her husband goes with another woman, since she has no rights in this matter. The law enshrines an extreme inequality of the sexes. Nor does it forbid husbands from having extramarital sexual relations, or forbid sexual relations between unmarried people; it merely forbids men from having sexual relations with other men's wives.[10] This is made clear by the passages parallel to the sixth commandment in Leviticus, which specify the offence as being committed by a man with the wife of his neighbor (Lev 18:20; 20:10).

Third, the law against bearing false witness does not enjoin general truthfulness. It forbids lying in court in a legal system which is heavily dependent on the word of witnesses. This system was known to be open to abuse, and this commandment is designed to minimize that abuse. Hence the law of Deut 19:15, which declares the word of one witness to be insufficient to secure the conviction of an accused; only if two or three witnesses agree is the charge sustained (cf. Jn 8:17f; Mt 26:59-61).[11]

Of course all these commandments are susceptible of a deeper interpretation from a Christian moral point of view; for this reason the decalogue has been accorded an important place in the tradition. But if such an interpretation presupposes Christian morality, it cannot without circularity be used to show that this morality has its basis in the decalogue. It is only the decalogue and other laws understood *in this way* that might begin to look like a basis for morality, but that Christians are to understand it in this way is not itself given in the law. The law has to be interpreted by what lies outside the law. What matters in the end is not so much the law itself as the way the law is interpreted and developed.

Law and Interpretation

This last point has implications for the insistence later on in the encyclical that there are certain negative commandments that may not be breached. It has been pointed out in discussion following the publication of the encyclical that even if this is accepted, to say that a particular negative commandment may not be breached is of little use until it is determined what counts as a breach. This in turn depends on how the commandment in question is interpreted. This problem has a biblical aspect to it, which

---

10. It is instructive to note the prudential arguments, given to a 'son', against adultery with another man's wife given in Proverbs 6:20-35 (esp. v. 26) and 7:4-27.

11. Even so the system could easily be used to work injustice, as in the story of Naboth's vineyard (1 Kgs 21:1-14).

the encyclical could profitably have dealt with. I have already mentioned Jesus's defence of his disciples when they are accused of profaning the sabbath (Mt 12:1-8). This repays closer attention. It should be noted that the sabbath law is neither a simple positive commandment nor a negative one. In its first statement it is positive: "Remember the sabbath day to keep it holy" (Ex 20:8; cf. Deut 5:12). But this is casted in terms of a negative precept: "In [the sabbath] you shall not do any work", etc. (Ex 20:10; cf. Deut 5:14). The division between positive and negative precepts is not as simple as all that. But how are we to interpret Jesus's defence of his disciples? Is he justifying their violation of the law prohibiting work on the sabbath, or denying that their actions constitute a violation? In fact he seems to be doing the former, for he speaks of the priests being guiltless despite their profanation of the sabbath (12:5); it is not that the priests do not profane the sabbath, but that they do and are nevertheless guiltless.[12] If we take this first alternative, we have Jesus himself declaring that a negative precept of the law ("You shall not do any work...") may be breached. This, it seems to me, is a problem for the encyclical which needed to be dealt with. If we take the second alternative, his words constitute an interpretation or reinterpretation of the sabbath law, one under which activities such as that of the disciples are permissible. This is less likely, but better for the thought of the encyclical. In fact it may be wondered whether it matters very much what we say here, whether the law does admit of breaches or whether the law itself is to be understood in such a way that this particular action does not constitute a breach. Though the encyclical insists throughout that the first option is to be ruled out, this seems to make little practical difference, as each individual precept still has to be interpreted; it has to be decided which actions are permissible under it and which are not. And it is not clear beforehand what are the limits of interpretation. That is to say, it is not obvious *a priori* what is the range of possible activities to be admitted under the law. What may seem legitimate interpretation to one person may seem a betrayal of the law to another, the legitimation of its violation, the evacuation of its content.

Thus in the succeeding pericope (Mt 12:9-14) we find just such a situation arising when Jesus faces a question about the interpretation of the sabbath

---

12. This interpretation would also be in line with Jn 5:17, in which Jesus does not attempt to deny a breach of sabbath law by healing, but justifies the breach. John also states in the following verse that Jesus broke the sabbath.

law. In the synagogue on the sabbath, when he is confronted by a man with a withered hand, he is asked by the Pharisees: "Is it lawful to heal on the sabbath?" (12:10). He argues from the fact that since animals may be rescued on the sabbath it is also lawful to heal, and proceeds to restore the man's hand (12:11-13). Clearly the Pharisees take a different view, since they now begin to plot to destroy Jesus (12:14). For them, Jesus's interpretation of the law amounts to no more than a specious justification of its violation. Here we have the reverse of the situation encountered in Mt 15:1-6, where Jesus characterizes the Pharisees' interpretation of a commandment as a specious legitimation of activities which in his eyes constitute a gross infringement of it. "God commanded 'Honor your father and your mother'.... But you say, 'If any one tells his father or his mother, what you would have gained from me is a gift to God, he need not honor his father'. So, for the sake of your tradition, you have made void the word of God" (15:4-6). This is an accusation which the Pharisees and scribes would no doubt have denied. We have no reason to suspect that the Pharisees were happy to disobey the law.

What emerges from the discussion of these passages from Matthew is that the insistence that certain precepts may not in any circumstances be breached is problematic (in view of Mt 12:1-8), and that it leaves untouched the real problem of deciding what may and what may not be done; it is to decide this that is the point of the biblical disputes between Jesus and the Pharisees. This point is not adequately recognized in the encyclical. This is not to say that it serves no purpose at all to insist that a simply-phrased precept may not be violated; it provides a focus for discussion of what is the will of God. The point I am making is that it is clear from scripture itself that the existence of a scriptural precept, whether positive or negative, does not settle the discussion about what may or may not be done but is only its starting point.

Intrinsic Evil

In chapter two of the encyclical the argument turns from general principles to more specific matters, the targets being "certain interpretations of Christian morality which are not consistent with 'sound teaching'" and "some trends of theological thinking and certain philosophical affirmations" (*VS*, 29). It turns out that among the trends that the encyclical has in mind are proportionalism and consequentialism. It is not for me to comment on whether these targets are well chosen, or on how successful the criticism of them is. I am concerned rather with how scripture is marshalled in the argument, and will concentrate on only one or two aspects of this.

One may have initial doubts as to whether scripture is directly relevant here at all. The argument over the acceptability of proportionalism and consequentialism as styles of moral thought is a modern one. It was not a live issue for either Old Testament or New Testament authors, nor for Jesus himself. We do not find Jesus in debate with the Pharisees about whether the consideration of consequences is a correct way to evaluate the moral status of an act.

Paul criticizes the Corinthians for priding themselves on being right (1 Cor 8:1f) and for not believing in the resurrection (1 Cor 15:12ff), but not for being proportionalists. If scripture is relevant at all to this debate, its relevance is indirect. Nevertheless, the encyclical does claim support for its position from scripture. Chapter two is almost as replete as any other part of the encyclical with scriptural references and quotations. How successful is the use of scripture here?

The instances of the use of scripture which I will look at are, I believe, the most important to the argument of the encyclical. In *VS*, 36 we find, towards the beginning of the attack on proportionalism and consequentialism:

> These trends of thought have led to a denial, in opposition to Sacred Scripture (cf. Mt 15:3-6) and the Church's constant teaching, of the fact that the natural moral law has God as its author, and that man, by the use of reason, participates in the eternal law, which it is not for him to establish.

At this point, at least, the claim that these trends of thought are opposed to scripture is supported by but one reference. And this reference turns out to be to Jesus's criticism of the Pharisees and scribes for transgressing the commandment of God for the sake of their tradition, which we glanced at earlier. For present purposes it is to be noted that there is in fact no accusation to be found here that the Pharisees deny that God is the author of the natural moral law, nor that they deny that human beings participates in the eternal law, nor that they claim that human beings can establish this law. Neither is there any such accusation in the Markan parallel (Mk 7:9-

13; Luke, generally unconcerned with law, has no direct parallel to this passage.) Indeed, there is nothing here about natural law or its authorship. Jesus's criticism of the Pharisees and scribes is that in their detailed application of the law as they have interpreted and developed it they have ended by promoting transgression of the commandment to honor one's parents, or evacuating it of its content.

Part of the argument against proportionalism and consequentialism takes the form of an insistence that there are 'intrinsically evil acts'. Biblical support is sought here. Thus *VS*, 79 is headed "'Intrinsic evil': it is not licit to do evil that good may come of it (cf. Rom 3:8)", and this same verse of Romans occurs in a quotation from St Thomas Aquinas on the inadequacy of judging the moral worth of an act from the intention of the agent alone (*VS*, 78) and from Paul VI on the illegitimacy of doing evil that good might come (*VS*, 80). It is not for me to comment on the use of Rom 3:8 in the tradition to which Aquinas and Paul VI contribute, but it is clear that Paul's argument in Romans 3 is not concerned with intrinsic evil. Paul does indeed seem to say that an evil act may not be performed that good may follow, but he has nothing to say here about the grounds on which an act is determined to be evil. He is not engaged in any debate about the grounds of moral judgement; he is not conducting an argument against consequentialists or their first-century equivalent. As far as the argument of Romans 3 is concerned, an act could be evil because it is intrinsically so, but it could also be rejected as evil on proportionalist grounds. Paul only says that if an act is evil - on whatever grounds - you are not to do it that good may come of it. Further, what consequentialists or proportionalists presumably want to say is, in any case, not that an evil may be deliberately done for the sake of its good consequences, but that an act may be good (or evil) in virtue of its consequences. Such a moralist would therefore be untouched by this use of Romans 3.[13]

---

13. If I may be permitted a wider comment on the traditional use of Rom 3:8, it seems to me doubtful whether what Paul says here really is relevant, as it has been regarded in the tradition, to the idea that one may not do one, evil, thing in order to bring about another, good, thing. What Paul seems to mean by good coming of evil is not achieving a good aim by evil means, bringing about a good change in the world by bringing about another, bad, change. Paul is talking about bringing about only one change - the commission of an evil act. God, the claim seems to be, is thereby put in a good light: "our wickedness serves to show the justice of God" (3:5). But showing the justice of God is not a *further* change. If you have an unpainted canvas and paint one half of it in a dark color you thereby make the other appear

While it may be implicit, there is no explicit claim here that the doctrine of the existence of intrinsically evil acts is taught by Paul in Romans 3. A little later in the encyclical, however, there is an explicit claim that this is a biblical doctrine.

> In teaching the existence of intrinsically evil acts, the Church accepts the teaching of Sacred Scripture. The Apostle Paul emphatically states: "Do not be deceived: neither the immoral, nor idolaters, nor adulterers, nor sexual perverts, nor thieves, nor the greedy, nor drunkards, nor revilers, nor robbers will inherit the Kingdom of God" (1 Cor 6:9-10). (*VS*, 81)

Note that the teaching about the existence of intrinsically evil acts is not said to be *derived* from what scripture says; it *is* itself a biblical teaching, according to the encyclical. The scriptural evidence offered for this assertion is slender and, it seems to me, insufficient. Note first that Paul is not talking about acts here at all, but people. From some of the people in the list - the greedy, drunkards, thieves - it seems as if he is talking of people for whom some act is habitual; the tendency to commit this act has become a defining part of their character. Paul appears to be speaking here not of the transgression of negative precepts, but of the acquisition of vices, the moral framework from within which he is speaking closer to a virtue ethic than to a legal one. This is supported by v. 12, where we find what appears to be a quotation from his own teaching which has been misused in the church at Corinth: "All things are lawful for me". Paul does not reply to this by asserting that, on the contrary, some things are unlawful, but replies in terms of the utility of actions and their relation to freedom. Secondly, he does not tell us why a habit of committing such acts debars one from the kingdom of God. In particular, he does not say that it is because they are habits of committing acts which are intrinsically evil. He may consider a habit of, for example, theft bad because of the consequences which acts of theft in general have, both on the victim and on the agent. As in Romans 3 so here, Paul is not engaged here in a theoretical argument against proportionalists or their first-century equivalent.

---

lighter by contrast. But you have not made two changes: painting one half dark and making the other appear light by contrast. The second is only a relational change. The darkening of one half is not a means to an end but itself part of the end, which is a situation of contrast.

This discussion of the argument of chapter two has been brief, but its brevity reflects the relative lack of weight placed upon scripture in this part of the encyclical. Although the scriptural references here are many, the purpose of most of them does not appear to be structural, or at least they are not central to the structure of the argument, which appeals fundamentally to considerations which are extra-biblical. It appears to me that it is only those discussed above that have anything approaching a central role. Most of the scriptural work has been done in chapter one. If I am correct in my assessment of the argumentation there, its scriptural basis is questionable and flawed in more than one way. Pope John Paul has performed an important service in stressing again that scripture is the fundamental source of Christian morality; but the particular way in which he has used that source is imperfect. It is at best a partial view of the moral teaching of scripture, and the pope's specific concerns - the inadequacies of certain modern moral theories - are not reflected in scripture. This is not, of course, to say that those concerns are not justified; but the particular justification sought for them in scripture is not to be found.

Summary of citations and references to Scripture in Veritatis Splendor

	Intro	Ch. 1	Ch. 2	Ch. 3	Conclu	Total
Genesis	1		5	3		9
Exodus		7	2			9
Leviticus		2		1		3
Deuteronomy		2	1	2		5
Joshua				1		1
Psalms	2	1	5	2	2	12
Proverbs			1			1
Wisdom		1	2	1		4
Sirach			3	1		4
Isaiah		1		2		3
Jeremiah		2	1			3
Ezekiel		2				2
Daniel			1			1
Joel				1		1
Amos			1			1
Micah		1	1			2
Matthew		43	12	11	2	68
Mark	1	5	2	4		12
Luke		11	1	5	3	20
John	5	24	7	9	3	48
Acts		2	2	4		8
Romans	1	11	20	4		36
1 Corinthians		7	3	4		14
2 Corinthians			5	3		8
Galatians		8	6	4		18
Ephesians	1	4	2	7	3	17
Philippians	1	2		2		5
Colossians	1	3	1	1		6
1 Thessal.	1		1	1		3
1 Timothy		1	1	2		4
2 Timothy	1		3	2		6
Titus			3			3
Philemon				1		1
Hebrews	1		1	1		3
James		1	2			3
1 Peter	1	1		1		3
1 John		6		8		14
Revelation		3		3		6
Totals	17	151	93	92	14	367

Teleology and Proportionality:
Thoughts about the Encyclical
Veritatis Splendor

Louis Janssens

An important part of the second chapter of the encyclical *Veritatis Splendor* (*VS*, 71-83) bears the title, "The Moral Act". The content addressed in this section is signaled with the subtitle, "Teleology and teleologism". Commenting on moral theologians who substantiate moral decisions teleologically and place significant weight in the concept of proportionality, the encyclical says, "*The teleological ethical theories (proportionalism, consequentialism)*, while acknowledging that moral values are indicated by reason and by Revelation, maintain that it is never possible to formulate an absolute prohibition of particular kinds of behavior which would be in conflict in every circumstance and in every culture, with those values" (*VS*, 75). In other words, they would deny "that the universal negative norms are binding for each and every person, at all times (*semper et pro semper*) and without exception" (*VS*, 52 & 75), or, what amounts to the same thing, they would be denying the existence of "acts which, in the Church's moral tradition, have been termed intrinsically evil (*intrinsece malum*): they are such *always and per se*, in other words, on account of their very object, and quite apart from the ulterior intentions of the one acting and the circumstances" (*VS* 80).

The papal document thus accuses these theologians of being trapped in an unacceptable ethical relativism. Although this allegation has been repeated for several years, I had thought that it had already been sufficiently answered. It therefore surprises me that the encyclical still puts forth these labels in reference to which no Catholic moral theologian will recognize as their own work.

Proportionality

Human "acting" means being engaged with reality. If that reality is material - because of our corporeality and the material realities of the world - then our activity is characterized by ambiguity. We can use the material things of the world in keeping with their specific nature and laws in order to achieve our goals, but we do not sufficiently control the consequences of this process to avoid disadvantageous effects for ourselves, other persons and the community. It is true that the progress of science and technology has increased our control of the material reality in and around us. But the ambiguity is not overcome. On the contrary, surgery, for instance, can save lives, but it simultaneously attacks bodily integrity. Can one think of medication that contains no side effects? Our laws attempt to regulate traffic in an efficient and safe manner, but they cannot prevent accidents. Dense traffic attacks the environment and literally thousands of (working) hours are lost in traffic jams. When I was a child, every new factory that was built was accepted unquestioningly as a good thing, the source of employment and the guarantee of more goods becoming available to more people. However, no one foresaw that industrial growth would have the effects that we now see in the air, the water and the ground. The ambiguous effects of the use of nuclear energy have become graphically clear in the Chernobyl disaster as well as in the problems of what to do with radioactive waste. It seems that the more we can control the material elements of our existence, the more ambiguity there is in our activity.

These facts make an appeal to proportionality unavoidable for evaluating the morality of human acts. An excellent example of this manner of thinking can be found in the "Declaration on Euthanasia," published by the Congregation for the Doctrine of the Faith on 5 May 1980 (*Origins* 10 [1980] 154-157).

The title of the fourth part of this document already says a good deal: "Due Proportion in the Use of Remedies." The document presumes that everyone has the duty to look after oneself or to look after others, which includes applying the appropriate remedies and therapies that have proven to be useful. Then it is asked whether one is obliged to use every single remedy that might be available. The classic response of the moral theologians was that one is never obliged to use "extraordinary" means. According to the Declaration,

> ...this reply, which as a principle still holds good, is perhaps less clear today by reason of the imprecision of the term and the rapid progress made in the treatment of sickness. Thus some people prefer to speak of "proportionate" and "disproportionate" means.

The Declaration thus adopts this manner of thinking.

> In any case, it will be possible to make a correct judgment as to
> the means by studying the type of treatment to be used, its degree
> of complexity or risk, its cost and the possibilities of using it, and
> comparing these elements with the result that can be expected,
> taking into account the state of the sick person and his or her
> physical and moral resources.

This form of argumentation constitutes a teleological foundation for moral
judgment: the deciding factor is the result that one can expect for the
patient. As one considers each and every advantage and disadvantage of
a treatment independently, one can still say nothing about the morality of
the event in its totality. Therefore, we describe these elements as *pre*moral
values and disvalues. At the same time we call them pre*moral* because they
are relevant to the moral judgment of our activity: one must consider the
totality of advantages and disadvantages in order to decide whether the
contemplated remedies will constitute a proportionate means to achieve the
hoped for result.

In order to demonstrate how to apply these general principles, the
Declaration provides a few concrete examples.

1. Treatment may be terminated when the expected results are not
achieved. To reach this conclusion one needs to consult the desires of the
patient as they were expressed at a time of relatively little stress; then, one
will also seek the advice of the family; but one also needs to consult the
advice of a competent doctor who can ascertain "that the investment in
instruments and personnel is disproportionate to the results foreseen, they
may also judge that the techniques applied impose on the patient strain or
suffering out of proportion with the benefits which he or she may gain from
such techniques."

2. No one is obliged "to have recourse to a technique which is already in
use but which carries a risk or is burdensome." Among the reasons that
the patient can have for refusing such a treatment, the declaration mentions
"a wish to avoid the application of a medical procedure disproportionate
to the results that can be expected or a desire not to impose excessive
expense on the family or the community."

The moral judgment about our dealing with the *material reality in and around us* is established teleologically, by considering all of the premoral values and disvalues that are involved in our activity and determining whether they are proportionate to the result that we are attempting to achieve. Even the moral quality of the result is determined teleologically. For example, every therapy is ideally aimed at the health of the patient, toward the restoration of the wholeness of the person. But in order to determine the extent to which any therapy should be applied, according to the declaration one needs to take into account "the state of the sick person and his or her physical and moral resources."

Teleology and Proportionality in the Thinking of Thomas Aquinas

In its approach to the moral analysis of human action, the encyclical frequently refers to texts of St. Thomas. Thomas takes as his point of departure the inner act of the will, the principle of each moral act, and he emphasizes the priority of the end, the specific object of the will. This is what is original in the approach of Thomas. According to Aristotle, a human act is willed in such a way that its origin (*arché*) lies in the one who is acting, a person who has knowledge of the *circumstances* of this particular act (*Eth.* 1. 3, c. 1). John Damascene speaks as well about the knowledge of the particular elements (*singularia*) through and in which human activity takes place, and these *singularia* he explains by invoking the classic list of *circumstances* (*De fide orthodoxa*, 1. 2, c. 24). Thomas names both these sources. But he introduces a change in their description that manifests his original way of thinking. *Voluntarium* is that which proceeds from the will (*S.T.*, I-II, q. 6, a. 3: voluntarium dicitur quod est a voluntate). In order to genuinely proceed from the will, the principle of the act must be interior (in the acting subject) and there must be a certain knowledge of the *end* (*S.T.*, I-II, q. 6, a. 2: ad rationem voluntarii requiritur quod principium actus sit intra cum aliqua cognitione finis).

Here Thomas distinguishes two forms of the knowledge of the end. The kind of knowledge that would be typical of animals he calls imperfect: through the use of their senses and their natural abilities, animals apprehend the reality that constitutes the end, but they have no understanding of the end or of the relationship between the action and the end. At the point that they apprehend an end, they are driven to achieve that end without further consideration. Human persons not only apprehend the reality of the end, they also have a comprehensive understanding of the end and the relationship between the end and that which needs to be done in order to achieve it (*cognoscitur ratio finis et proportio* eius quod ordinatur in finem ad ipsum ... *proportio* actus ad finem). What is more, in contemplating an end, a person may consider not only the end itself but also that which must be done in order to achieve that end, and only then decide whether one wants to perform the action. (*S.T.*, I-II, q. 6, a. 2).

From his description of the *voluntarium*, it appears that Thomas proposes the priority of the end of our activity. He works teleologically. When a person actually decides to work toward realizing an end, this means that he or she has already willed the means necessary to achieve that end (actus, ea quae sunt ad finem), a means that is capable of realizing that end and "proportionate" to the end. This proportion refers to the fact that in each case the action is of such a nature that the end can genuinely be realized and, morally speaking, does not stand in contradiction with the moral value of the end (*S.T.*, I-II, q. 18, a. 4, ad 2: debita proportio ad finem).

Final End and Proportionality

According to St. Thomas, moral theology must first deal with the final end of human life and only after this can it deal with those things by which persons achieve this end, for it is from the end that one determines those things that are oriented toward that end (*S.T.*, I-II, q. 1, Introductio). Clearly, this is a teleological perspective. In this final end, Thomas distinguishes the *finis cuius*, or the reality which is the end itself, namely God, and the *finis quo*, or the reaching of the end (adeptio, consecutio finis) and this takes place in knowing and loving God (*S.T.*, I-II, q. 1, a. 8). As a theologian, he refers to love as *caritas* (amor caritatis), which is a gift of the Holy Spirit (*S.T.*, II-II, q. 23, a. 2) and which directs the person toward the highest good: the enjoyment of God (*S.T.*, II-II, q. 23, a. 7). At the same time, he brings our attention to the fact that the object of *caritas* is God, the neighbor, and oneself (*S.T.*, II-II, q. 23, a. 2). This *caritas* is the principle of our spiritual life: "The end is the principle of our actions. Consequently, the love for God and for neighbor - the end of our human activity - is the principle of our spiritual life that is present in the goodness of our actions" (*De Malo*, q. 7, a. 1).

The object of an action is a real good (vere bonum) when it stands in the right relationship (proportio, ordinatio, commensuratio) with the demands of love;

it is only an apparent good (bonum apparens) if it stands in contradiction (repugnantia, contrarietas, exclusio) with love.

This is how Thomas summarizes his understanding of the right orientation of the will (rectitudo voluntatis) and at the same time the differentiation between the formal and the material elements of human activity:

> Rectitude of the will consists in being duly ordered to the last end (debitum ordinem ad finem ultimum). Now the end in comparison to what is ordained to the end (id quod est ad finem) is as form compared to matter. Wherefore, just as matter cannot receive a form, unless it be duly disposed thereto (nisi sit debito modo disposita ad ipsam), so nothing gains an end, except it be duly ordained thereto (debito modo ordinatum ad ipsum). And therefore none can obtain one's final end (beatitudo), without rectitude of the will. (*S.T.*, I-II, q. 4, a. 4)

According to Thomas, we must judge the whole of our lives, everything we do and choose not to do, teleologically. Charity - as *finis quo* - is the formal element of all virtuous actions (in actibus omnium virtutum est formale id quod est ex parte caritatis). For the material elements of our actions to be ready to receive the formal elements, our actions must be virtuous (*Quaestio disp. de caritate*, q. unica, a. 3; II-II, q. 23, a. 8, II-II, q. 88, a. 2; nec aliquod opus sit Deo acceptum nisi sit virtuosum). Only in this situation do we find the 'debita proportio ad finem'.

Teleology and Proportionality in Particular Acts

From the very beginning of his moral theology, Thomas asks the question whether the end determines the moral goodness or badness of our actions. He answers that, in fact, our action receives its moral species - its being good or bad - from the end (actus morales *proprie* speciem sortiuntur ex fine). The realization of the end is only achieved when the action is completed. However, the end is first in the intention of the acting person and as such it is the object of the will and determines the moral character of human actions (*S.T.*, I-II, q. 1, a. 3 in corpore, and ad 2). Nevertheless, we should not forget that in the same article 3, ad 3, an important distinction is noted:

One and the same act, in so far as it proceeds from the agent, is ordained to but one proximate end (finis proximus), *from which it has its species*: but it can be ordained to several remote ends (fines remoti), of which one is the end of the other.

According to Thomas, the specific difference between a morally good and a morally bad act is determined by the object in accordance with its relation to reason (*De Malo*, q. 2, a. 5: actus moralis speciem habet ex obiecto secundum ordinem ad rationem; cfr. I-II, q. 18, a. 2). Analogous to his hylomorphic theory of reality, Thomas speaks of the formal and the material elements in the object of an action: "The object determines the species (moral goodness or badness) of the act, not according to the material element that is present (non secundum id quod est materiale in ipso), but according to the formal quality of the object" (*De Malo*, q. 9, a. 2, ad 10). The object is not only the material in which the act consists (non est materia ex qua), but the material with which one actively works (materia circa quam); as such, the object has the quality of the formal element that determines the moral nature of the action (*S.T.*, I-II, a. 18, a. 2, ad 2). The object of an action must be described in such a way that it can be determined whether it is in accord with reason and is therefore *conveniens* or *inconveniens*. From the examples that he gives, it appears that Thomas tried carefully to define the object of the action. One of his examples is the specific difference between *cognoscere suam* and *cognoscere non suam*, sexual relations with one's wife and sexual intercourse with a woman with whom one is not married. In both cases there is coitus, according to Thomas an *actus naturalis*, the identical material element. However, the formal element, the relationship with reason, is determined by the *sua* and the *non sua*, so that the two actions are specifically morally different (specie differunt secundum quod sunt actus rationis ... prout sunt *actus morales*). In the case of sexual intercourse, then, one's own wife is 'obiectum conveniens' and the act is morally good (as long as the circumstances are acceptable) while a woman who is not one's wife is 'obiectum inconveniens' and the act is called adultery, a term that designates an immoral event (*De Malo*, q. 2, a. 4 in corpore and ad 6).

When one speaks of the object of an act, what is referred to is the *exterior action*. An action can only be human (actus humanus) and moral when it proceeds from the will (voluntarium). In order to determine the morality of an action, then, Thomas begins with the *inner act of the will* of which the proper object is the end. In this perspective, the object of the exterior action is the immediate end (finis proximus) that is willed by the subject. "Insofar as one considers the exterior action (in executione operis) then one relates it to the will as an object that has the quality of an end" (*De Malo*, q. 2, a. 3). In any given action, one can distinguish between an end that is close and an end that is distant: "The immediate end (finis proximus) of an act is the same as its object, and it is on the basis of this end that the act receives its moral species" (*De Malo*, q. 2, a. 4, ad 3). In his *Summa Theologia*, Thomas sums up this perspective in the following way:

> Objects, in relation to external acts, have the character of matter *about which* (materia circa quam); but, in relation to the interior act of the will, they have the character of end; and it is owing to this that they give the act its species. Nevertheless, even considered as the matter *about which* (materia circa quam), they have the character of term, from which movement takes its species (*Phys*. v., *Ethic*., x. 4); yet even terms of movement specify movements, insofar as term has the character of end. (*S.T.*, I-II, q. 72, a. 3, ad 2).

In this last sentence, Thomas considers action as a dynamic event (motus) that has its origin in the inner act of the will, and within which the will activates all the dynamic elements until the purpose is fulfilled (the finis proximus). An action in which the finis proximus is morally bad is fundamentally immoral and cannot be made good by any remote end, however good that end might be. If the finis proximus is morally good, but the real reason (causa) behind the action is an immoral finis remotus, then the inner act of the will makes the entire event morally bad (cfr., *S.T.*, I-II, q. 18, aa. 2, 6 & 7; q. 75, a. 4).

Thomas, therefore, arrives at the moral judgment of particular actions teleologically. From this it follows that whatever is done in order to achieve a goal (ea quae sunt ad finem) must be proportionate to that goal and thus must not be in contradiction to the moral value that is present in the goal itself. The fact that this is Thomas' position can be illustrated by the way in which he deals with concrete cases.

The goal or purpose of human laws is the common good of the society.

> Whatever is for an end should be proportionate to that end (fini
> proportionatum). Now the end of law is the common good....
> Hence human laws should be proportionate to the common good
> (proportionatas ad bonum commune). Now the common good
> comprises many things. Wherefore law should take account of
> many things, as to persons, as to matters, and as to times.
> Because the community of the state is composed of many persons;
> and its good is procured by many actions. (S.T., I-II, q. 96, a. 1)

Thomas poses the question whether it is justifiable to kill someone in a case
of self-defense. The goal, namely the protection of one's own life, is
morally justified and may thus function as the object of the intention of the
one who is defending oneself. But the action that flows from a good
intention can be improper, such as when it is not proportionate to the end
(si non sit proportionatus fini). Therefore, it is condemnable to use more
force than is necessary in order to defend one's life. In other words, as
long as one defends oneself through the use of force which is proper
(moderato, cum moderamine inculpatre tutelae) to the situation in which
one must hold off the attack of one who threatens us, there is a proper
proportion between the end and the means (S.T., II-II, q. 64, a. 7).

To illustrate that the theologian must take account of the circumstances of
human action, Thomas proposes the following as the first reason.

> The theologian considers human acts, in as much as a person is
> thereby directed to his final end (beatitudo). Now, everything that
> is directed to an end should be proportionate to that end
> (proportionatum fini). But acts are made proportionate to an end
> by means of a certain commensurateness (secundum commensur-
> ationem quandam), which results from the due circumstances.
> (S.T., I-II, q. 96, a. 1)

One must consider the entire action. Thus, the circumstances are also
relevant in order to judge whether an action demonstrates the proper
relationship (proportio) to the morally good end.

Intrinsically Evil Acts According to Their Object

Aristotle already had a clear notion about actions that are intrinsically immoral (in se).

> The very name of some actions immediately indicates that they are morally bad, such as adultery, stealing, murder. These and other such actions have a bad name because they are immoral in themselves.... In these cases, it is impossible to act well. What one does is bad. The circumstances have no influence on their goodness or badness. If one commits adultery, it is meaningless to ask whether this occurred with the right woman or at the right moment or in the right manner, for to do such a thing is bad. ... Such actions are bad, no matter how they are done. (*Nic. ethic.*, 1, 2, c. 6)

Following Aristotle, the medieval theologians repeat that one can immediately say that certain actions are certainly (in se, per se) immoral by the very way in which they are named, for their name points in the direction of something immoral.

No one can deny that there are acts that are intrinsically bad on the basis of their *finis proximus*. However, this presumes that the object of these acts has already been carefully determined in a teleological manner. Let us consider some examples.

Stealing is an intrinsically evil act. In order to determine that, however, one must first ascertain what the object of such an act is before it can be called stealing. Theologians have traditionally taught that God has directed the goods of the earth for the benefit of all. That is their fundamental purpose, for without using the goods of the earth life is impossible. Thomas says that after the fall, the ordering of this universal use is indispensable, and he considers private ownership as a means for guaranteeing this ordering. This is a teleological foundation that supposes that private ownership enjoys the *proper relationship* toward the fundamental right to the use of all things that make life possible. On the basis of a goal-directed right to private property, Thomas concludes that in a situation of extreme need (urgens, extrema necessitas) one may take that which one needs from another's property when there is no other means to guarantee that which is needed to sustain one's life. "The action is, in the real meaning of the word, not stealing; for in such a situation of need what one takes in order to maintain one's life is actually one's own." Thomas adds that one may also take from the property of another in secret in order to help a neighbor who is in a similar need (*S.T.*, II-II, q. 66, a. 7 and ad 2 and 3). It is clear that Thomas bases his understanding of the object of stealing teleologically.

Murder is an intrinsically bad act because of its object. But when should the killing of a person be called murder? Morally speaking, what is the object of murder? The life of a person is a fundamental value, for it is only when persons are living that the other values can be realized. That said, the moral theological tradition has always accepted that the killing of persons is not always equivalent to murder. The argumentation in this respect has also always been teleologically founded. In the case of licit self-defense, one appeals to the right to life and claims that the right to protect one's life is a morally responsible end, even if this entails the death of one's attacker as the only possible means to achieve that end. Similarly capital punishment is considered justifiable when it appears to be necessary for the protection of the greater value of the common good. In order to defend the freedom and the independence of its citizens, it has been taken for granted that a country may commission its soldiers to fight against and even kill the enemy. The judgment that, in each one of these cases, killing is not identified with the object of murder is clearly founded upon a teleological basis.

There is also the delicate, and thank goodness very infrequent, case in which the removal of a non-viable foetus is necessary in order to save the life of the mother, when no other possible means are available. In such a case there is but one alternative for the medical profession. Either nothing is done and both mother and foetus die (omissio); or the foetus is removed (commissio) and the life of the mother is saved, the only life that can be saved in this situation. Teleologists will judge the active medical intervention to be morally right, for the end of the medical profession is to practice in the service of life, and in this instance the saving of one life is chosen over the loss of two lives.

Thus we agree with Aristotle and the medieval theologians who followed him in saying that we can immediately grasp the meaning of specific actions such as adultery, rape, torture, stealing, murder, and so forth, always being immoral. The naming of these acts, however, not only tells one what occurs but that what is occurring is immoral. At the same time, this judgement is only possible because the object of such actions is described teleologically.

The Object Adequately Considered

The encyclical draws attention to the fact that it remains necessary to do research in order to determine the norms for moral living in a coherent manner and to validate these norms with rational arguments (*VS*, 74). A growing number of moral theologians are convinced that this determination must be founded upon a teleological basis. In social ethics this constitutes a normal state of affairs. In that area, no one doubts the virtue of teleological reasoning. However, when it comes to sexual ethics many people think that teleological reasoning is insufficient and that another form of argumentation is necessary. Should we therefore consider having two types of moral theology, one for social questions and another for sexual issues?

Official church documents maintain that contraception, homologous artificial insemination, masturbation, sterilization and homosexual acts are intrinsically evil according to their object. All of these terms refer simply to factual events. Using Thomistic categories, one could say that they designate only the material element of the object (id quod est materiale in ipso, materia ex qua), while only the formal element, namely, the way in which human persons relate to reality (materia circa quam) provides sufficient information for judging whether a human action is reasonable and thus morally responsible. Or, to put it in more concrete terms, how can we judge whether the actions performed by human persons really and objectively promote the human, personal subject as a relational reality?

In the case of legitimate self-defense, is it morally responsible to strive for the protection of one's own life? This end of the subject is the formal element of the object of the action. This is evident from the fact that the force that is used, the material element of the object, can only be considered morally justifiable to defend oneself when it stands in the correct (proportionate) relationship with the end to be achieved, that is, one does not use more force than is necessary for achieving that end. Only in this case can this action be justified on the basis of a personalist ethic. As a personal subject the human being has a right to life and may defend that life with the appropriate means. As a relational being, the person respects his or her relationship with the attacker in that one only uses the amount of force that is morally responsible. Simultaneously, one's relationship with the community is morally right, for an important element of the common good is to protect innocent life and in the case of legitimate self-defense the acting person is the representative of the community.

Lying is intrinsically bad according to its object. But what is the object of lying? Saying something that is untrue (falsiloquium) is not always equivalent to lying (mendacium). For instance, if someone tries to filch a professional secret from a person, that person may have no option for protecting the professional secret other than telling an untruth. The end of the person, the protection of the professional secret, is the formal element of the object of the action that justifies what is done, even when, of necessity, telling a falsiloquium constitutes the material object of the act. As a subject, one fulfills a responsibility as the keeper of a professional secret. One has acted correctly toward the person who was attempting to acquire information to which that person had no right. One serves the community by protecting professional secrecy because without this protection there would be a lack of trust perpetuated that would undermine the professional relationship.

From these examples it appears that the end toward which the subject strives in each case is not merely an element of the object of the action but the formal element that is so important that it determines whether the material element of the object is *materia debito modo disposita*. In my opinion, this holds true for issues in sexual ethics as well; as in all the other cases, the moral decision is teleologically based.

Take, for instance, the case of homologous artificial insemination. Determining whether such a procedure provides the only possible manner of achieving pregnancy is the task of a medically competent person. In order to arrive at a moral evaluation of such a procedure, however, the theologian will need to ask whether the use of such a procedure truly functions to promote the human persons who are associated with the event, persons who are subjects, in corporeality, who stand in relation with the whole of reality. The moral theologian will attempt to substantiate the presumption that there is a genuine conjugal love between the spouses that will sustain the relationship that is necessary for the successful bringing up of the child. If these conditions are fulfilled, I suggest that a potential pregnancy and birth could aptly be characterized as, according to *Gaudium et Spes*, the ultimate crown of marriage and conjugal love (*GS*, 48) and the supreme gift of marriage that contribute substantially to the welfare of the parents (*GS*, 50).

Even if it is brought into existence through homologous artificial insemination, the child is still the fruit of marriage. It has come into existence in the context of marriage and owes its life to the contribution of two persons who are committed to each other. They are the true parents of the child. At the same time, the child is the fruit of conjugal love; it has been wished for through the mutual love of a man and woman. The pregnancy is welcomed with the shared joy of both partners. One can easily understand how such things can be characterized as teleological. They clearly achieve the promotion of the persons who are concerned in these matters.

For the spouses, the child is "a supreme gift of marriage that contributes very substantially to the welfare of the parents" (*GS*, 50). At the same time, as subjects in corporeality, their sexual relations remain an expression and a support of their love (*GS*, 48). Particularly in their situation, it is important that they remain conscious of the relational meaning of their love for each other. For the child, it is salutary to know that both parents wished to being it into existence and that the mutual love of its parents is the source of their decision to procreate and to educate this new life. As social beings, the parents also bear a responsibility for the good of society. They contribute to this by insuring that stable marital relationships thrive and blossom into family life.

I suggest that with this sort of teleological thinking we are very distant from the fear that technical help with homologous artificial insemination will "transform the family hearth which is the sanctuary of the family into a mere biological laboratory" (Pius XII, "Address to the Midwives," *A.A.S.*, 43 (1951) 835-854).

In order to accomplish this project, an act of masturbation on the part of the husband is necessary. The term masturbation refers only to the factual description of what takes place (materia ex qua), the material element of the object of the action. The end that one has in mind with this act, however, is the formal element of the object of the act. In the case where pregnancy is not achieved within a marriage in the normal manner, the question about infertility arises and an act of masturbation will be necessary in order to determine whether the male partner is infertile. Before artificial insemination became possible, this act of masturbation could not be considered to be procreative. In light of contemporary technological achievements, however, one could even consider masturbation as an action in direct service to the achievement of procreation.

In our active commerce with material reality - our corporeality and the material realities around us - the morality of our actions is to be judged teleologically, by examining whether the totality of their elements are proportionate to the attainable good result. This result is morally good if it promotes the involved persons adequately considered as subjects in corporeality and as relational realities. The Declaration on Euthanasia is a striking example of this teleological approach. It is clear that all actions concerning sexuality involve corporeality. Is it not then the case that, in a coherent moral theology, the same holds true in the domain of sexuality, so that the morality of these actions are to be judged teleologically?[1]

1. This article was translated by Joseph A. Selling.

Erroneous Conscience in *Veritatis Splendor* and the Theological Tradition

Brian V. Johnstone

The encyclical *Veritatis Splendor*[1] deals with the question of erroneous conscience in paragraphs 62-63, within the context of the treatment of conscience and truth in paragraphs 54-64. The aim of this article is to analyze the encyclical's teaching on erroneous conscience and to situate it in relation to the wider moral theological tradition. This may facilitate a better understanding of the meaning and import of that teaching.

In the relevant paragraphs, the text reflects the influence of a very important school of theology.[2] However, there have been a variety of schools of thought in Catholic moral theology which, while agreeing on many matters, have differed on certain important points. Some of these schools have been influential in the Church for centuries and have been approved by the Magisterium[3] or at least have never been officially rejected, and would seem to have made a positive contribution on some matters. A secondary aim of this chapter is to make a case for the continuing theological validity and usefulness of at least some of these other schools of thought. While the document reflects one theological approach in particular, it does not reject all others. Indeed, it is clearly stated that, "Certainly the Church's Magisterium does not intend to impose on the faithful any particular theological system, still less a philosophical one" (*VS*, 29). It is therefore appropriate to consider these other schools and explore their place in the moral theological tradition as a whole.

---

1. Vatican City: Libreria Editrice Vaticana, 1993. The document will be cited henceforth as *VS* with the paragraph number.

2. St. Thomas Aquinas is cited twice in the footnotes, and the influence of his thinking is clearly evident. St. Bonaventure is cited once.

3. For example, the theology of St. Alphonsus Liguori has been given papal approval, specifically by Pope Pius IX who, on March 23, 1871, conferred on him the title of doctor of the Church. Also noteworthy is the very significant tradition associated with theologians of the Society of Jesus.

This essay has three parts. The first will analyze official texts from the documents of the Second Vatican Council, the *Catechism of the Catholic Church*,[4] and the encyclical *Veritatis Splendor*, which deal with erroneous conscience. It will be demonstrated that these documents themselves show differences and tensions. The second part will identify the major issues which have occasioned these differences. The third part takes up each issue and situates it in the context of the wider theological tradition.

Three Authoritative Texts on Erroneous Conscience

The principal conciliar text which deals with conscience is, of course, paragraph 16 of the "Pastoral Constitution on the Church in the Modern World," *Gaudium et Spes*.[5] The final text was the result of compromises between widely differing schools of thought.[6] The text itself also allows for different interpretations of some basic statements, some giving primacy to law,[7] others to more personalist considerations.[8] It is noteworthy that some parts of the conciliar text on conscience are omitted in the corresponding text of the Catechism. The first instance does not seem to be particularly significant. The Catechism (1776) omits the following statement concerning

---

4. The French version of the document, *Catéchisme de l'Église Catholique*, 2nd. ed. (Paris: Mame-Librairie Editrice Vaticane, 1992) will be cited, with the paragraph number. The English translation is by the author.

5. *A.A.S.* 58 (1966) 1037. English translation from *Decrees of the Ecumenical Councils*, Vol. 2, ed. Norman P. Tanner (London and Washington: Sheed & Ward and Georgetown University Press, 1990) 1077-1078. Where the English version of *VS* cites a conciliar text, the *VS* translation will be used.

6. Domenico Capone, "Antropologia, coscienza e personalità," *Studia Moralia* IV (1966) 93-113; Karl Golser, *Gewissen und Objektive Sittenordnung: Zum Begriff des Gewissens in der Neueren Katholischen Moraltheologie* (Vienna: Wiener Dom Verlag, 1975) 123. Cf. Josef Fuchs, "Was heißt 'irriges' Gewissen?" *Stimmen der Zeit* 211 (1993) 797.

7. Martin Rhonheimer, *Natur als Grundlage der Moral* (Innsbruck: Tyrolia, 1987) 35. The author cites T. Styczen, "Das Gewissen - Quelle der Freiheit oder Knechtung?" *Archiv für Religionspsychologie* Bd. 71 (1986) 130-147.

8. Eberhard Schockenhoff, *Das Umstrittene Gewissen: Eine theologische Grundlegung* (Mainz: Grünewald, 1990) 107-8.

the law which is written by God in the heart: "To obey it is the very dignity of man; according to it he will be judged" (*GS*, 16).[9] (A)

However, others are more noteworthy. Omitted from the Catechism is the section of *GS*, 16, which reads:

> In a marvelous manner conscience makes known that law which is fulfilled by love of God and of neighbor. In their faithfulness to conscience, Christians are united with all other people in the search for truth and in finding true solutions to the many moral problems which arise in the lives of individuals and in society. (B)

The contents of this passage, however, provided an important modification of earlier drafts.[10] The immediately following text from *GS*, 16 is, however, included at the end of the Catechism's section on conscience (1794): "And the more a correct conscience prevails, so much the more do persons and groups abandon blind whims and work to conform to the objective norms of morality."

The Catechism omits the statement of *GS*, 16 which, in the conciliar text, comes after this, namely: "not infrequently conscience can be mistaken as a result of invincible ignorance, although it does not on that account forfeit its dignity;"[11] (C) For this text, there is substituted an interesting variation: "But it happens that conscience is in ignorance and makes erroneous judgments... (1790). This ignorance can often be imputable to personal responsibility" (1791).[12] However, the sentence which, in *GS*, 16 immediately follows "dignity" is included: "(but this cannot be said) when

---

9. Translation from *VS*, 54.

10. The introduction of the theme of love of God and neighbor in the final text qualifies what would otherwise have been a one sided emphasis on natural law. Another significant change was also introduced, Christians are said to be linked with others *fidelitate erga conscientiam* rather than, as in the earlier text, *huius legis lumine*. See Golser, *Gewissen*, 128; Capone, "Antropologia," 108.

11. Translation from *VS*, 62.

12. "Mais il arrive que la conscience morale soit dans l'ignorance et porte des jugements erronés. . .Cette ignorance peut souvent être imputée à la responsabilité personnelle."

a man shows little concern for seeking what is true and good, and conscience gradually becomes almost blind from being accustomed to sin " (1791).[13] The closest parallel, in the Catechism, to the omitted conciliar text on dignity is: "The dignity of the human person implies and requires rectitude of conscience " (1780).[14]

The omitted texts, (B) and (C) derived from one particular modus which was accepted into the final document.[15] The omission of these particular passages may have been due simply to a concern to avoid undue length. However, the text of the Catechism, as it stands, shows a preference for an interpretation which gives priority to law over conscience, and favors a submissive model of conscience.

We must now turn to the relevant passages in *Veritatis Splendor*. There are different models of conscience evident in the document. The "religious" model understands conscience in terms of a dialogue between God and the human person; accordingly guilt is not merely guilt before the law, but guilt before God.[16] This notion is clearly reflected in the text (*VS*, 58). However, a strongly objective, intellectual model is also present. The following text may be taken as an example: "... whereas the natural law discloses the objective and universal demands of the moral good, conscience is the application of the law to a particular case " (*VS*, 59). This model shapes the encyclical's interpretation of conscience and influences the way in which the question of erroneous conscience is treated.

It is interesting to note that the encyclical cites two of the three passages from *GS*, 16, which have been omitted from the Catechism.[17] In particular,

---

13. Translation from *VS*, 62.

14. "La dignité de la personne humaine implique et exige *la rectitude de la conscience morale.*"

15. For the modus see *Acta Synodalia SS. Concilii Oecumenici Vaticani II*, Vol. IV, Pars VII, (1978) Correctiones Admissae, Ad num. 16, pp. 317-318. On the modus see Golser, *Gewissen*, 218, n. 41; and Capone, "Anthropologia," 97, 98, 108, n. 16. For the text incorporating the modus see *Acta, loc. cit.,* p. 244.

16. Cf. Golser, *Gewissen*, 117.

17. *VS*, 54 cites (A); *VS*, 62 cites (C); (B) however, is not cited.

VS, 62 quotes that passage from *GS*, 16 which acknowledges that conscience frequently errs through invincible ignorance, although it does not thereby loose its dignity. Indeed, according to the encyclical, in this statement and the following sentence, which says that this does not apply to one who is not concerned for truth, and whose conscience becomes almost blinded by sin, "... the Council sums up the doctrine which the Church down the centuries has developed with regard to the *erroneous conscience*." It is surely significant that the encyclical has taken up again this particular text and included it in the summary of Church doctrine.

The Major Issues Concerning Erroneous Conscience

In this section we indicate the most important topics and analyze the way in which they are presented in the official texts.

Why Does Erroneous Conscience Bind?

According to *VS* the authority of conscience derives from the "...truth about moral good and evil" (*VS*, 60). Furthermore, conscience, even when in (invincible) error, speaks "... in the name of that truth about the good" (*VS*, 62). The phrase "in the name of" recalls the earlier citation from St. Bonaventure, calling conscience "God's herald" (*VS*, 58) and suggests the metaphor of the proconsul and the emperor which is cited by St. Thomas, who himself cites St. Augustine. This metaphor was used to explain why one should obey conscience, even if it is in error. Thus, if a person believes the command of the proconsul is the command of the emperor, then when one treats with contempt the command of the proconsul, one shows contempt for the command of the emperor.[18] What would seem to need further explanation is why the proconsul (conscience) must be taken to speak in the name of the emperor (God). Further, how is it that conscience still "speaks" in the name of God, when the judgment which conscience delivers is not, in fact, in accord with the law of God? It is noteworthy that the text does not invoke St. Thomas' solution that erroneous conscience binds "per accidens".[19] The problem of the foundation of the obligation of erroneous conscience, has been a difficult one for the

---

18. *S.T.*, I-II, q. 19, a. 5, ad 2.

19. *De Veritate*, q. 17, a. 4.

theological tradition and it would not seem, as yet, to have found a completely adequate solution.

The Moral Status of the Act which Follows on Erroneous Conscience

The encyclical states that "the evil done as the result of invincible ignorance or a non-culpable error of judgment", remains an evil, and cites a text of St. Thomas in support of this (*VS*, 63).[20] St. Thomas' view was that involuntary ignorance, while it renders the *will* not bad, does not make the *act* good.[21] However, there is in the tradition, another school of thought, according to which the act which follows upon erroneous conscience could be said to be, in some sense, good and the person performing the act could be judged to be good.[22] What was the basis of this opinion and how does it differ from the position of St. Thomas? To answer that will require an investigation into the theological tradition.

The encyclical acknowledges that, "It is possible that the evil done as a result of invincible ignorance or a non-culpable error of judgment may not be imputable to the agent" (*VS*, 63). St. Thomas holds that if the error of conscience is truly involuntary, then it excuses. Thus the will which is in accord with the erroneous reason is not evil.[23] It would seem to follow that where the error is truly involuntary, it is inculpable, and that an objectively wrong act which was performed according to this error is not imputable to the agent.[24] In short, in such a case, not only is it *possible* that the evil

---

20. *De Veritate*, q. 17, a. 4.

21. Dalmazio Mongillo, "Interpretazione della dottrina tomasiana sulla coscienza," *La coscienza cristiana*, ed. Leandro Rossi (Bologna: Dehoniane, 1971) 58. Cf. *S.T.*, I-II, q. 19, a. 6.

22. James F. Keenan, "Can a Wrong Action Be Good? The Development of Theological Opinion on Erroneous Conscience," *Église et Théologie* 24 (1993) 205-219.

23. *S.T.*, I-II, q. 19, a. 6.

24. See Dennis J. Billy, "The Authority of Conscience in Bonaventure and Aquinas," *Studia Moralia* 31 (1993) 256: "(Thomas) argues that it is sinful to follow our mistaken reason only when the mistake is the result of voluntary ignorance. (I-II, q. 19, a. 6) In the case of perplexity, if the ignorance is involuntary, then the resulting action does not fall in the moral area: if it is voluntary, then there is nothing to prevent the person from shedding that

may not be imputable, but it *is* not imputable.[25] In fact, the Catechism states without qualification that, where the ignorance is invincible or the erroneous judgment is not culpable, the evil committed cannot be imputed to the person (1793).[26] Does the encyclical intend to take a more restrictive position than St. Thomas himself? To deal with this question we need to explore what the tradition has had to say concerning the nature of the error of conscience which may remove imputability.

The Range of Inculpable Error

St. Thomas indicates two distinct kinds of error. One is where the error concerns a circumstance, and in this case the (involuntary) error of conscience excuses. The other is error about the law of God which one ought to know, in which case the error does not excuse. Here, however, the error is voluntary since one is negligent; one does not will to know what one ought to know.[27] An involuntary error excuses; but a voluntary error does not excuse. But if the error excuses, it would seem to follow that the evil done as a result of the error is not imputable to the agent. The qualifications "possible" and "may", therefore, remain puzzling.[28]

The document may intend to imply that it is conceivable that a person could perform an evil act in "invincible ignorance" and yet be guilty, since the ignorance may have originally been brought about by sin. That would mean that ignorance could be here and now invincible, but still at root culpable.[29] Indeed the text suggests just such an idea: "There are faults which we fail

---

voluntary ignorance."

25. St. Thomas uses the language of "excuse" rather than "imputability". It is not clear how we should understand the relationship between the terms. St. Thomas discusses imputability in connection with grace and conversion. See *Summa contra Gentiles*, III, 159.

26. "... le mal commis par la personne ne peut lui être imputé."

27. *S.T.*, I-II, q. 19, a. 6.

28. "It is possible" may perhaps been intended to mean something like "even granted that..." The Italian text has "può", the German "kann", the French "peut".

29. *VS*, 62 defines invincible ignorance as "an ignorance of which the subject is not aware and which he is unable to overcome by himself."

to see but which nevertheless remain faults, because we have refused to walk towards the light" (*VS*, 63). If this is what is meant, then it would make sense to say that it is merely "possible" and not necessarily so, that the evil not be imputed when it is the result of invincible ignorance. That is to say, the evil would not be imputed where the invincible ignorance was in no way culpable; but it would be imputed if the ignorance were culpable, that is the result of sin.

However, even if the text intends to allow for the possibility of invincible ignorance which is culpable, the basic difficulty in understanding the passage still remains. The non-imputability of the evil done, is said to be possible (rather than necessarily so), also in the case of "non-culpable error". As has been shown, this is difficult to explain in terms of the theological tradition, and specifically in view of the teaching of St. Thomas. It is, therefore, difficult to provide a satisfactory explanation of this part of the text. However, the discussion has raised the question of "sins of ignorance" and this notion calls for some elucidation in relation to the theological tradition.

Elsewhere St. Thomas allowed for the possibility of ignorance regarding the secondary principles of the natural law, and recognized that some principles called for more subtle argument and for instruction.[30] These statements were later cited in support of the possibility of accepting a wider range of inculpable error.[31] It is not clear whether the encyclical intends to adopt a more restrictive interpretation of the range of error or whether it would allow such a broader view.

The Nature of Moral Truth

The document presents three levels of truth; the objective truth in itself, the declaration of that truth in reason, and finally its recognition in the judgment of conscience (*VS*, 61). The truth attained by conscience here is simply a recognition of an already given ontological reality, which is the ultimate criterion. The encyclical however, also includes the notion of

---

30. *S.T.*, I-II, q. 94, a. 6; cf., I-II, q. 100, a. 3.

31. St. Alphonsus Maria De Ligorio, *Theologia Moralis*, 9th. ed., Leonard Gaudé, vol. I (Rome: Typographia Vaticana, 1905) lib. I, tr, 2, cap. 4, dub. 1, n. 171, pp. 148-149.

sincere seeking for the truth: "... that truth about the good which the subject is called to seek sincerely" (*VS*, 62). That to which the person is called is not precisely to attain the truth, but rather to seek it sincerely. Seeking implies activity of the will, and sincerity expresses the idea of "good will". Thus we seem to have an alternative notion of moral truth, namely conformity of conscience to good will.[32]

It has been noted that a religious model of conscience is also represented in the encyclical. The language of *VS*, 58[33] reflects *GS*, 16 which speaks of conscience as the secret core of man, where one encounters God, or hears the voice of God.[34] According to this interpretation, conscience is not primarily an experience of a law or an impersonal ontological order, but the experience of a personal relationship with God. *VS*, 64 identifies the "heart" which is converted to God, as the source of true judgments of conscience. Truth is thus founded on an affective co-naturality. These considerations suggest a third notion of moral truth, namely correspondence to a personal relationship, founded on affectivity.

A related question concerns conscience and prudence. An extended discussion of the topic would be beyond our scope, but since it has a bearing on moral truth, a comment is needed. The conciliar text does not mention prudence.[35] The Catechism refers to "... the prudent judgment of conscience" and says that the person is called prudent who chooses in conformity to this judgment (1780). In one short paragraph (*VS*, 64) the encyclical brings together elements of a doctrine on prudence which scholars recognize are essential for an adequate notion of conscience.[36] Including the notion of prudence enables us to move beyond an

---

32. This seems to reflect not so much the Thomist tradition, as a later Suarezian variant.

33. The text derives from an address by Pope John Paul II, *Insegnamenti*, VI, 2 (1983) 256.

34. This text derives from Pius XII and was introduced into the final text via the modus indicated in note 15. See Golser, *Gewissen*, 218; Capone, "Anthropologia," 97.

35. *GS*, 15 mentions wisdom and the gifts of the Spirit, but not prudence.

36. Terrence Kennedy, "L'idea di coscienza morale secondo S. Tommaso d'Aquino," *La coscienza morale oggi*, ed. Marian Nalepa and Terrence Kennedy (Rome: Academia Alphonsiana, 1987) 169-171; Mongillo, "Interpretazione," 48.

understanding of conscience, which interprets it only in terms of the application of law, and similarly enables us to transcend the opposition of law and conscience which characterized much of the theology of the manuals. The personal moral self does not stand as unformed freedom before an imposed and constricting law. Rather the self is formed and oriented by "virtuous attitudes" towards the true good, including the theological virtues (*VS*, 64). The biblical language of the "heart" is invoked together with the metaphysical language of the good, to indicate the source and criterion of true judgments of conscience. Thus the moral life is construed as a continuous movement towards the good, or as a "continuous conversion". This is a very important paragraph as it sets conscience in its proper moral and religious context.

The Status of Conscience and therefore of the Person, in Invincible Error

What is the significance of the statement that conscience, even when in (invincible) error, retains its dignity? The text of the Catechism would seem to imply that when conscience is not "right" it does not have dignity (1780).[37] The encyclical, however, relates dignity to *seeking* sincerely or striving towards the truth (*VS*, 62). Thus dignity does not have an exclusively objective basis, but can be founded on personal *subjectivity*. This more personal, subjective element is an interesting complement to the otherwise firmly objective account of conscience, which we find in the encyclical.

The preceding analysis has indicated that on a number of points the official texts themselves differ and so raise questions which need to be answered. The next step will be to situate each of these points in the wider theological tradition. The aim here is both to seek answers to these questions, and to show that some of the other traditions may help in providing those answers.

---

37. According to the Thomist tradition conscience is said to be "right" (*recta*) when it is in accord with the objective truth. However, according to a second tradition, conscience could be said to be "right" even in the case where it is not in accord with objective truth, but is in error in good faith. See Louis Janssens, *Liberté de conscience et liberté religieuse* (Paris: Desclèe de Brouwer, 1964) 24. If the rectitude of conscience were understood in this second way, dignity would imply and require either true conscience or erroneous conscience in good faith.

Erroneous Conscience in the Theological Tradition[38]

Why Does Erroneous Conscience Bind?

According to St. Thomas, the will has access to the good, which is its object, only through the mediation of reason.[39] The source of all obligation is the eternal law of God. Reason is the necessary mediator of that law to the agent. Therefore, reason or conscience mediates the obligation to the agent. Similarly, if there is no mediation of knowledge, there is no obligation.[40] Conscience, however, according to St. Thomas, binds not because it proclaims an obligation arising from itself, but rather one which comes from the eternal law of God. It is an obligation imposed definitively by God, who is the end and true good of the human person.[41]

We can now deal with the specific question: Why and how does *erroneous* conscience bind? St. Thomas explains that the will which is in discord with erroneous conscience (reason) is bad because of its object. The relevant object here is not that object as it is by its own nature, but as it is (in this particular situation, "per accidens") apprehended by reason. In this situation, reason apprehends that object as evil. If then the will moves towards that object, the will becomes evil.[42] St. Thomas' position was revolutionary in relation to the state of the tradition at his time.[43]

The position is perfectly clear. However, we may ask whether all questions have been answered. How can it be that conscience, in the case where it does not mediate the eternal law, that is where conscience is in error, still

---

38. For an extended account see Golser, *Gewissen*, 39.

39. *Quaestiones Quodlibetales, Quodlibetum* 3, q. 12, a. 2 [27].

40. *De Veritate*, q. 17, a.3.

41. Mongillo, "Interpretazione," 55-56.

42. *S.T.*, I-II, q. 19, a. 5.

43. Richard Heinzmann, "Der Mensch als Person: zum verständnis des Gewissens bei Thomas von Aquin," *Das Gewissen: Subjektive Willkur oder oberste Norm?* ed. Johannes Gründel (Düsseldorf: Patmos, 1990) 50.

communicates the obligatory power of that law? Some commentators accept St. Thomas's argument as convincing.[44] Others find it incomplete.[45] The criticism is made that the notion of obligation "per accidens" is a poor compromise, and does not succeed in synthesizing the objective morality, given by the object, and the personalist understanding of morality which Thomas himself proposes.[46]

Consider the following examples of arguments which have been put forward. Suarez sought to solve the problem by proposing that conscience, including invincibly erroneous conscience has its binding force, not from objective law, but from conscience itself.[47] Zalba takes up the phrase "per accidens" and explains it to mean that invincibly erroneous conscience binds on the basis of ignorance which grounds the false, but prudent, conviction of the law and its obligation.[48] Others believed a better explanation was needed. Fuchs sought to address this difficulty on the basis of an analysis of moral reasoning.[49] Mongillo argues from the ontology of the moral order.[50] Karl Rahner sought to explain the absolute binding force of erroneous conscience on the basis of a transcendental experience of the subject, of freedom and responsibility, which is present even when one errs regarding the categorical object.[51] Heinzmann seeks an answer in terms of

---

44. Servais Pinckaers, *L'Evangile et la morale* (Fribourg, Switzerland: Editions Universitaires, 1990) 268.

45. Cf. Timothy Potts, *Conscience in Medieval Philosophy* (Cambridge: Cambridge University Press, 1980) 60.

46. Golser, *Gewissen*, 45.

47. Franciscus Suarez, *Omnia Opera*, t. IV (Paris: Vivès, 1856) disp. XII, sec. II, 5, p. 440; Régis Araud, "Le 'Traité de la Conscience' chez Suarez: Analyse de la Conscience," *Science et Esprit* 20 (1968) 68; Janssens, *Liberté*, 15; Carlo Caffara, "Il concetto di coscienza nella morale post-tridentina," *La coscienza cristiana* (ed. Rossi) 75-104; Golser, *Gewissen*, 51.

48. *Theologiae Moralis Compendium*, vol., 1 (Madrid: 1958) 370.

49. Golser, *Gewissen*, 137.

50. Mongillo, "Interpretazione," 58.

51. Karl Rahner, "Vom irrenden Gewissen," *Orientierung* 47 (1983) 248-9.

the dignity of the person.[52] There is a serious question here, to which no generally accepted answer has yet been given. Thus the proposed solutions of the various schools need to be considered and weighed carefully.

We now need to consider an important branch which has emerged with the tradition. That tradition which stems from St. Thomas understands conscience as fundamentally an organ of communication with the divine law.[53] The tradition continues from St. Thomas, through St. Alphonsus, to the Dominican school of the present century.[54] However, while St. Alphonsus followed St. Thomas in his account of conscience as communication, he diverged, or at least adopted a particular, and controversial interpretation of St. Thomas on one important point. This concerned the moral status of the act which followed from the erroneous conscience. This issue calls for comment.

The Moral Status of the Act which Follows on Erroneous Conscience

As has been noted, according to St. Thomas, involuntarily erroneous conscience does not make the act good, but renders the will not evil.[55] William of Ockham (d. 1350) went beyond St. Thomas on this point, arguing that not only does involuntary ignorance excuse from sin, but the will eliciting an act in conformity with (invincibly) erroneous reason is virtuous and meritorious.[56] Although he does not cite Ockham, St. Alphonsus follows this position, arguing that one who acts with an invincibly erroneous conscience not only does not sin, but probably acquires merit.[57] St. Alphonsus states that on this point he follows

---

52. Heinzmann, "Der Mensch," 50.

53. Eberhard Schockenhoff, "'Testimonium conscientiae,' Was ist norma proxima des sittlichen Urteils?" *Der Streit um das Gewissen*, ed. Gerhard Höver and Ludger Honnefelder (Paderborn: Schöningh, 1993) 74

54. Schockenhoff, "Testimonium," 74.

55. *S.T.*, I-II, q. 19, a. 6.

56. *III Sent.*, q. 13, C. See Michael E. Baylor, *Action and Person: Conscience in Late Scholasticism and the Young Luther* (Leiden: E. J. Brill, 1977) 87.

57. *Theologia Moralis*, vol. I, lib. 1, tr. 1, n. 6, p. 4.

Fulgentius Cuniliati, O.P.,[58] together with others "communissime". He did not, therefore, claim to be propounding a new doctrine.

St. Alphonsus accepts that such an act is not "in se" right.[59] Thus he does not claim that the act itself is somehow changed in its material nature.[60] Alphonsus uses both "right" and "good" of the act. The act can be said to be right according to the conscience of the agent.[61] It can also be said to be good,[62] at least inadequately, since to be good it suffices that it be directed by reason and prudence. When an agent acts prudently he or she earns merit, on account of the good end for which he or she acts, namely the glory of God and the good of the neighbor. On the contrary, one would loose merit, who does a good work, apprehended as evil, because of the evil end for which the act was done.

Alphonsus takes up the obvious objection, namely that according to St. Thomas, good arises from an integral cause, but bad from any defect.[63] Thus, for an act to be good, it must be both good by reason of its nature, and apprehended as good. Alphonsus replies that St. Thomas was speaking of the good absolutely and simply, and not of the good considered relatively, as apprehended by conscience in its condition of invincible ignorance.[64] Here Alphonsus considered that he was taking to its logical conclusion, the basic position of St. Thomas, namely that the act is to be

---

58. Fulgentio Cuniliati, *Universae Theologiae Moralis Accurata Complexio*, pars 1a. (Venice: Dominicus de Mazo, 1796) 3.

59. *Theologia Moralis*, loc. cit., n. 5, p. 4.

re not sins in the true sense of the word. They are called material because they would be the matter of sin if they were committed with advertence that they were sins. See Domenico Capone, "Realismo umano-cristiano della teologia morale," *Studia Moralia* 9 (1971) 87-104; Golser, *Gewissen*, 66; 191.

61. *Theologia Moralis*, loc. cit., n. 5: "...juxta conscientiam operantis."

62. *Ibid.*, n. 6; n. 7.

63. *S.T.*, I-II, q. 19, a. 6, ad 1.

64. *Theologia Moralis, loc. cit.,* n. 7; "... respective et per accidens prout a conscientia, quae est regula proxima agendi, invincibiliter apprehensum est..."

judged virtuous or vicious according to the good as known (*bonum apprehensum*) to which the will is directed, and not according to the material object of the act.[65] The teaching of Alphonsus on erroneous conscience was widely accepted by moral theologians in the 19th century and into the present.[66] His position was taken up for example by Gury,[67] Ballerini,[68] Ferreres,[69] Noldin,[70] Aertnys-Damen,[71] and others.

These authors did not of course mean to say that, because the agents were invincibly ignorant of the sinfulness of the acts, that the acts they performed (for example, stealing or lying) were not objectively wrong. They simply accepted that certain acts were "in se" that is, in themselves, morally wrong. They then went on to deal with the moral condition of the agent, and her or his spiritual condition in relation to God.[72] The thinking of these authors was shaped by the practice of the confessional, where major considerations were the moral and spiritual condition of the penitent, and therefore the determination of the responsibility of the penitent for her or his acts.[73] Moral theologians presumed that human acts could be judged

---

65. *Quodlibetum*, 3, q. 12, a. 2.

66. The development of this tradition is well described by Keenan, "Can a Wrong Action be Good?" 214.

67. Joannes Petrus Gury, *Compendium Theologiae Moralis* (Lyons: Perisse, 1850) n. 36, p. 25.

68. Joannes Petrus Gury, *Compendium Theologiae Moralis*, 10th. ed. Antonio Ballerini, vol. I (Rome: Civiltà Cattolica, 1866) nn. 36-38, p. 43.

69. Joannes B. Ferreres, *Compendium Theologiae Moralis*, t. 1, 11th. ed. (Barcelona: Eugenius Subirana, 1921) nn. 93-95, pp. 52-54.

70. Hieronyous Noldin, and Anton Schmidt, *De Principiis Theologiae Moralis* (Regensburg: Fel. Rauch, 1931) n. 212, p. 210.

71. Joseph Aertnys, *Theologiae Moralis Secundum Doctrinam S. Alfonsi De Ligorio*, t. I, 11th., ed. C A. Damen, (Turin: Marietti, 1928) nn. 51-53, p. 42.

72. Cf. Aertnys-Damen, *Theologia Moralis*, p. 42.

73. Joseph A. Selling, "*Veritatis Splendor* and the Sources of Morality," *Louvain Studies* 19 (1994) 3-17, 14.

"in themselves". They then engaged in an extended analysis of the individual's accountability. A problem arose here in that theologians confused "... an approach for determining guilt and responsibility with a normative analysis of human actions in themselves."[74] It was only at a later stage of development within the tradition that moral theologians were able to clearly distinguish between the analysis of individual accountability and a normative moral theory concerning the rightness and wrongness of acts.[75] This lack of a clear distinction may have given rise to serious misunderstandings within the tradition. It would seem that some moral theologians have continued to work within the paradigm which has just been explained. Thus they may acknowledge that certain acts "in se" are (materially) wrong, but allow that the moral condition (striving) of the person (with inculpably erroneous conscience) is right or good. Where this latter analysis is confused with the normative analysis of human actions, these theologians appear to be proposing a theory of "double truth" or "double status of moral truth" (cf. VS, 56). Specifically, they may appear to be saying that, while a particular act is wrong "in itself", in respect to the person's concrete condition, it may be right. However, the second affirmation is not properly a statement about the act, but rather about the person's moral condition. Thus, we do not have a double truth about moral acts, considered under the same aspect. Rather, we have an affirmation of truth about the status of the act, and a distinct affirmation of truth about the moral condition of the person. Furthermore, the model of moral truth which operates in the first case is that of conformity to the objective order, while in the second case the model is that of correspondence to right striving. It is, therefore, most important to recognize that moral truth is not a univocal, but an analogous notion. On the other hand, these moral theologians may not always have made it clear that they are analyzing the moral condition of persons, or accountability, and not developing and applying a normative theory of the rightness and wrongness of acts. A clear distinction between the different operations may help to resolve some serious difficulties in this area.

We can consider now the statement of the encyclical that the evil done following a judgment of erroneous conscience remains an evil or disorder

---

74. Selling, *Veritatis*, 14.

75. Selling, *Veritatis*, 15.

(*VS*, 63). The language used here recalls that of St. Thomas, who distinguishes *malum, peccatum*, (a disordered act) and *culpa*.[76] The moral theologians we have mentioned previously would, of course, accept the statement of the encyclical that the act resulting from erroneous conscience remains a *malum*, and a *peccatum*. An evil remains an evil. Even when it follows from an invincibly erroneous conscience, a disordered act remains disordered.

However, as has been pointed out, those theologians who held that the act which followed on an invincibly erroneous conscience could be said to be "right" or "good" in some sense, or "formally" good, were asking a different question. They were concerned not only with the physical evil done, or the correspondence or lack of it, between the material act and the objective law (which they presumed), but also with the moral orientation of the subject, or with the total spiritual relationship of the subject to God. That is, they were inquiring about *culpa*. These questions do not replace or render unnecessary the task of establishing how the rightness or wrongness of acts should be determined. However, they are distinct and valid questions which need to be asked.

The Range of Inculpable Error

St. Alphonsus accepted what he considered to be the common opinion, namely that conscience could be in invincible error concerning the precepts of the natural law, not indeed the first principles or the immediate and proximate conclusions drawn from them, but the mediate and remotely derived conclusions.[77] The authors of the manuals took a similar view. They discussed the cases where a person steals to help another, being invincibly ignorant of the wrongness of the act of stealing, or under similar conditions lies to protect someone else.[78] Thus, the moral theological tradition came to accept this relatively wider range of error.

---

76. *De Malo*, q. 2, a. 2.

77. *Theologia Moralis*, loc. cit., n. 8.

78. See e.g. Benedictus H. Merkelbach, *Summa Theologiae Moralis*, vol. II, 8th. ed. (Bruges: Desclée De Brouwer, 1949) p. 52.

However, not all manualists of the past accepted this. There was a rigorist school exemplified by Daniele Concina (1687-1756) who hesitated to accept that there could be inculpable error even concerning the remote conclusions of the natural law.[79] Most cases of erroneous conscience he believed to be instances of vincible, culpable ignorance. For him there are sins of ignorance, and they are many. From these convictions he drew the somber conclusion that, probably, most Christians would be damned.[80]

What we have here is a version of the doctrine of "sins of ignorance" according to which I may sin unknowingly, that is without actually adverting to the sinfulness of what I am doing, because my lack of knowledge is due to earlier sin. Concina strongly defended this view.[81] Other theologians, including St. Alphonsus, held that actual advertence of some kind was necessary for mortal sin.[82] Accepted Church teaching, as presented in the Catechism states that mortal sin requires full knowledge and deliberation (1857).

A version of the doctrine of sins of ignorance can be found in some contemporary writing, notably in some reflections by Cardinal Joseph Ratzinger.[83] The Cardinal's thesis is that conscience may be blinded, as the result of a deliberate withdrawal from the truth, because one did not want to see.[84] The basic point is that conscience should not be reduced to a superficial, subjective certitude and misused as a way of avoiding facing the truth and one's guilt.[85] This is surely a valid concern. It seems reasonable to suggest that such

---

79. Golser, *Gewissen*. 64; Daniele Concina, *Ad Theologiam Christianam Dogmatico-Moralem Apparatus*, t. II (Rome: Occhi, 1751) diss. II, cap. III, n. 58, p. 116.

80. Golser, *Gewissen*, 64.

81. *Ad Theologiam*, diss. II, cap. IV, p. 127.

82. *Theologia Moralis*, vol. II, lib. V, *De Peccatis*, cap. 1, dub. 1, n. 4, p. 707.

83. Joseph Ratzinger, "Gewissen und Wahrheit," *Ethos* Sonderausgabe, Nr. 1 (1993) 131-146, p. 137; "Coscienza e verità," *Idem. La chiesa: una communità sempre in cammino* (Milan: Paoline, 1991) 113-137, p. 118.

84. "Coscienza," 120.

85. "Coscienza," 121.

blindness could be a reality, for example in such persons as Hitler.[86]

There are, however, some further questions which Cardinal Ratzinger does not discuss. The first is of a more theoretical nature. Could such blindness be so complete as to exclude all awareness, and leave a person in a state of "invincible ignorance"? In St. Thomas' terms, as we have explained earlier, where one chooses not to seek the truth, or does not choose to seek the truth, the error of conscience would be voluntary, and would not excuse. But if it is voluntary, it would seem there must be some awareness; the blindness could not be total. *GS*, 16 acknowledges that conscience may be almost (fere) blinded by sin. But this implies that conscience would not be totally blind. There would, therefore, even in this extreme case, be some advertence to the wrongness of what one did. It would seem, therefore, that one could not, at the same time, be culpably ignorant, and have no awareness of this, that is be in "invincible ignorance".

The second question is of a pastoral, theological nature. The rigorist Concina seems to have thought that many, or even most, Christians, while being in what seems to be invincible ignorance, are in fact culpably ignorant. Are we to assume that many people are in this condition of culpable ignorance and are, without actual advertence, sinning? Both *GS*, 16 and the corresponding text of the Catechism (1790) acknowledge the reality of ignorance. But the respective estimates of the human condition appear to be different. According to *GS*, 16, people's consciences are "not infrequently" in a condition of invincible ignorance, although they do not loose dignity on this account. The implication is that the ignorance is often inculpable. As we have noted, the Catechism shifts the emphasis on this point: in its judgment, the ignorance can often be culpable (1791). The difference can be stated succinctly: Christians are often ignorant, but inculpably so; Christians are ignorant, but often culpably so. For the present it must suffice to note these differences within the tradition.

The Nature of Moral Truth

This is, of course, the central and most difficult matter of all. In the preceding analysis of the official texts, three models of truth were found. A review of the moral theological tradition in its contemporary form brings

---

86. "Coscienza," 118.

to light the same three models: (1) Moral truth is conformity between the conscience and the ontological order in the universe;[87] (2) Moral truth is conformity between the conscience and rightly ordered striving;[88] (3) Moral truth means the correspondence between conscience and the person's whole spiritual relationship with God. This would include the specifically moral element, but would be more comprehensive. It would appear that this was what some older authors had in mind when they proposed that an act which followed upon an invincibly erroneous conscience, was not only excused but meritorious. The same idea is presented by recent authors who employ more specifically religious and evangelical language when dealing with the question. Thus, rather than speaking of ontological order, they speak of "the mystery of Christ", and rather than the natural law, of the law of love of God and neighbor.[89] As has been noted, the encyclical itself (VS, 64) identifies the "heart" converted to the Lord as the basis of true judgments of conscience. Moral truth must then be regarded as an analogous notion. It would therefore be a mistake to accept only one model of truth, to acknowledge that as "objective" and reject all others as "subjective". The second and third models are not necessarily merely "subjective"; they concern the objective reality of the subject's moral orientation and relationship to God.

The encyclical does not discuss the relationship between conscience and prudence. This may well be because the debate on this point, within the tradition, has been intense and complex. Some authors who favor an objective-intellectual model of conscience emphasize that conscience is distinct from prudence, and that conscience does not coincide with the act of prudence.[90] Others, while insisting that prudence does not determine the

---

87. This expression is intended as an equivalent to the term "allgemeinverbindlich Seinsordnung." See Franz Furger, *Gewissen und Klugheit* (Lucern: Räber, 1965) 57.

88. See, for example, James F. Keenan, "Distinguishing Charity as Goodness and Prudence as Rightness: A Key to Thomas's *Secunda Pars*," *The Thomist* 56 (1992) 409; *Idem.* "Can a Wrong Action be Good?" 217.

89. Capone, "Anthropologia," 109.

90. Lèon Elders, "La doctrine de la conscience de saint Thomas d'Aquin," *Revue Thomiste* 91 (1983) 557; Ralph McInerny, "Prudence and Conscience," *The Thomist* 38 (1974) 303.

truth of conscience, see the two as complementary,[91] others again identify (right and certain) conscience and prudence, or argue that prudence determines the truth of conscience.[92] The positive contribution of *VS* is to affirm the role of prudence and thus broaden the theological discussion of conscience, a move which should be most fruitful. In this *VS* is reflecting an important revival within the Catholic moral theological tradition, recent fruitful, contemporary reformulations of the tradition,[93] and a growing interest in prudence in modern ethics.

The Status of Conscience and therefore of the Person, in Invincible Error

As has been noted, the citation of the text from *GS*, 16 in *VS*, according to which conscience in invincible error retains its dignity, would seem to indicate a move back from a strongly objectivist model to a more personalist understanding of conscience, as was reflected in *GS*. However, no doubt because of the fundamental concern with the contemporary rejection of or indifference to moral truth, and even the denial of the possibility of its attainment, the encyclical seems to be more concerned to stress the "truth about moral good and evil" (*VS*, 60) than to develop an integrated, personalist vision. Nevertheless, the elements of such a vision are present.

If a personal conscience retains its dignity, even when mistaken as the result of invincible ignorance, then conformity to an objective moral order alone cannot be the fundamental constitutive element of moral personhood. Further, if conscience is the vehicle of communication between God and the person, and it can remain such even when the content (i.e. the judgment) of conscience is not in accord with God's law, then there must be more to personal conscience than the transmission of correct judgments. Contemporary moral theologians have taught us to look not only at the conformity of acts to the ontological order, but to the goodness (or badness)

---

91. T.H. Deman, *La prudence, Somme Théologique*, II-II, 47-56, (Paris: Desclée, 1949) 505.

92. See Domenico Capone, "La 'theologia moralis' di S. Alfonso: Prudenzialità nella scienza casistica per la prudenza nella coscienza," *Studia Moralia* 25 (1987) 44, n. 44.

93. Keenan, "Distinguishing". Cf. Daniel Mark Nelson, *The Priority of Prudence: Virtue and Natural Law in Thomas Aquinas and the Implications for Modern Ethics* (University Park, Penn.: The Pennsylvania State University Press, 1992).

of persons, which is interpreted in terms of right striving, or "striving out of love for the right".[94] This is surely a valid line of inquiry which has emerged from one school within the moral theological tradition, and deserves respectful attention. Another promising avenue would be to explore more fully the language of personal dignity, and interpret conscience not in relation to an abstract, ontological order, but in regard to the ontology of the person.

Conclusion

The conclusion makes two points, one particular and one more general. The first is that the encyclical, while apparently allowing only one interpretation of erroneous conscience, does not require such a restriction. The second point is that some other schools still have theological relevance and validity in that they seek to answer questions which have not been adequately answered, or pose questions which need to be asked. The complexity of the issues and the range of diversity, even among official documents which deal with conscience, indicate that the theological interpretation of conscience is still in a process of development. Development involves diversity and conflict. However, this is what the history of the tradition would lead us to expect. Some might think of the Catholic moral tradition as necessarily a unitary tradition. Those who have such a conception of tradition find it difficult to accept that a living tradition will include a plurality of positions in conflict, and indeed that it must do so, if it is to continue to be a living tradition. The encyclical itself, in keeping with the venerable practice of the Church, recognizes plurality in its clear declaration that it does not intend to impose any particular theological or philosophical system. A living tradition is one which can allow diversity and allow itself to be questioned, because it is confident that it can respond to these questions, and in so doing, vindicate its truth.

---

94. Keenan, "Can a Wrong Action be Good?" 206.

Circumstances, Intentions and Intrinsically Evil Acts

Bernard Hoose

In an article written fairly soon after the publication of the encyclical, Richard McCormick made some complimentary remarks about *Veritatis Splendor*, acknowledging, for instance, that "all Catholic moral theologians should and will welcome the beautiful Christ-centered presentation unfolded in chapter one." He also pointed out, however, that the key second chapter is both dense and technical. In it, he notes, the pope has joined in "an in-house conversation among moral theologians." In order to deal adequately with the encyclical, he feels, one has to negotiate some very heavy theological literature. "Very frankly," says McCormick, "few non-specialists will read the papal letter, and of those who do most will emerge with cluttered and clouded but not clear heads."[1] I really have no idea how many people, specialists or non-specialists, have, by the time of my writing this chapter, made any serious attempt to read the encyclical; but I have noted signs of confusion among people who have read it and among others who have not read it, but who have heard about certain things therein from people who have. Much of what I want to deal with here is, in fact, contained in that dense second chapter. I shall attempt, therefore, to deal with the matters concerned as clearly as possible, so as not to pile confusion on confusion. It is perhaps only fair to warn the reader, however, that more than one enigma is likely to show its face in the course of our discussion.

Much of the confusion arising from reading the encyclical centers, it seems to me, around the concept of intrinsic evil, a concept which has apparently been dear to several recent popes in recent times, John Paul II obviously not being an exception. In fact, much of what follows concerns the pope's use of that concept.

---

1. Richard McCormick, "Killing the Patient," *The Tablet*, 247 (1993) 1410-1411, p. 1410.

Intrinsically Evil Acts

One sometimes hears conversations in which one party becomes rather exasperated with the other's apparent refusal to understand. Reacting to a particularly upsetting item that she has just read about in a newspaper, for instance, Margaret may declare that a certain type of action is always wrong. As is her wont, Tracy responds by describing a case in which that kind of action would most certainly not be wrong. Margaret clearly has in mind examples like the one she has just read about in the newspaper and feels sure that her companion is well aware of that fact. She therefore replies: 'You know perfectly well what I mean.'

The writers of *Gaudium et Spes*, one of the documents of the Second Vatican Council, apparently assumed that their readers would know what they meant when, in a section calling for respect for the human person, they presented a list of actions which they described as criminal.[2] In the second chapter of *Veritatis Splendor*, in a section dedicated to the moral act, John Paul II reproduces that list. One of the actions in it is deportation. It might therefore be claimed that it would be unfair to suggest that, merely because he describes all the actions in the list as intrinsically evil, the pope is thereby denying to governments the right to send back to their own countries foreign visitors who are clearly a danger to civil order and/or national security. 'Surely,' some might say, 'we know perfectly well what the pope means.' The matter, however, is not quite as simple as that. If we take seriously everything he says in this section - and he evidently wishes us to do so - it seems we have to conclude that, in his opinion, all deportation is wrong.

The very existence of this section, it would seem, can be attributed, in large part, to the pope's concern regarding at least some of the views held by a group of revisionist moral theologians who are sometimes referred to as proportionalists. These scholars, he says, hold that it is impossible to qualify an act as morally evil according to its object (*VS*, 79). That claim on the part of the pope touches the very center of much of what we have to discuss here. In order to understand, moreover, just what is being said in the second chapter of this encyclical, and in order to appreciate what is being said by the revisionist theologians to whom the pope is referring, it

---

2. *Gaudium et Spes*, 27.

would seem that we have to make some attempt to get to grips with the meaning or meanings being attributed to that word 'object'.

Some might say that the object of an action is the action itself considered apart from circumstances and intentions, but that does not make everything crystal clear. Let us take up the example of cutting someone with a knife. It could be said, and quite rightly, that even such a simple description of the object is not completely devoid of context. The fact that the cutting implement is some sort of knife is surely part of the circumstances. After all, we could cut the person with something other than a knife - our finger nails, for instance. Even if we take cutting with some form of knife - breadknife, scalpel, dagger, or whatever - to be the object, we clearly cannot judge the rightness or wrongness of a particular instance of this action without knowing something more about the morally relevant circumstances and the intention of the person acting. Is the cutting an act of war, for instance, or is it an act of self-defence, or part of a surgical operation? Even if we knew the answer to that question, we would still not know enough about the circumstances to be able to judge the moral rightness or wrongness of the act. Let us suppose, for instance, that it is an act of war. Even if the war is a just one, it does not follow that every aggressive act on the part of those involved in that war is a justified one. If it is an act of self-defence, it may, in the circumstances, be an exaggerated one. We do not know whether it is or not because we simply do not know enough about the circumstances. If it is part of a surgical operation, it may or may not be the case that the operation is an unnecessary one, or one carried out without the patient's permission.

Let us take up an example of the last mentioned of the possibilities, a surgical operation. Some years ago, Josef Fuchs discussed a case of kidney transplant, describing the removal of the kidney as the object.[3] In such a case, the fact that the person from whom the kidney is being removed is healthy is at least part of the circumstances, and the end or intention is a transplant of the kidney into the body of another person who needs it. It could be pointed out, of course, that the object here is more than merely cutting somebody with a knife. We could perhaps say, therefore, that, as acts get to be more and more complicated, so too may the objects of those

---

3. Josef Fuchs, *Essere del Signore: Un Corso di Teologia Morale Fundamentale* (Rome: Pontificia Università Gregoriana, 1981) 196.

acts become more complex. Some might say, and, indeed, rightly, it seems to me, that what is happening is that more circumstances are being absorbed into the object. Interestingly, moreover, in the work just referred to, Fuchs describes the removal of the kidney as the object *in the strict sense*. In order to decide on the rightness or wrongness of an action, he says, we need to know what he calls the total, or, alternatively, the entire, object, by which he means the object in the strict sense, plus circumstances and intention (or end).[4]

Apparently adopting a similar line of thinking, Richard McCormick, who, like Fuchs, is one of the leading proportionalists, says in the article referred to earlier that he believes all proportionalists would admit that some acts are intrinsically evil from their object *"if the object is broadly understood as including all the morally relevant circumstances."*[5] Here lies the center-point of quite a large problem, for the pope does indeed claim that there are acts which are intrinsically evil, but goes on to say that

> ... they are such *always and per se*, in other words, on account of their very object, and quite apart from the ulterior intentions of the one acting and the circumstances. Consequently, without in the least denying the influence on morality exercised by circumstances and especially by intentions, the Church teaches that "there exist acts which *per se* and in themselves, independently of circumstances, are always seriously wrong by reason of their object". (*VS*, 80)

To keep matters clear, let us return for a moment to the case of kidney transplant. One has the impression that, a long time ago, many Catholics would not have been opposed to all removing of kidneys from corpses. After all, they were accustomed to sending bits and pieces of bodies around the world as relics of the saints. One could well imagine, however, that a point might have been reached - at least for those who were opposed to the hanging, drawing and quartering of witches, heretics and criminals - in which they would have described the removal of a kidney from a healthy person as always morally wrong, or, if you prefer, as an intrinsically evil

---

4. *Ibid*. Emphasis mine.

5. Richard A. McCormick, "Killing the Patient," p. 1411. Emphasis his.

act. In parenthesis, so to speak, we should perhaps note that circumstances have been added to the removal of the kidney (the fact that the person is healthy). Now, let us assume, for the sake of argument, that the highest authorities in the Church are among the ranks of those about whom we have been talking and that they are considering the object thus described when they say that such an act is intrinsically evil and that no additional circumstances can render such an action morally right. A statement like that might seem to be correct until somebody comes up with the idea of transplant surgery. In other words, additional circumstances can render morally right an act that, in most other circumstances so far experienced by humans, would be morally wrong.

John Paul II, however, is apparently confident that this cannot happen with any of the actions in the list borrowed from *Gaudium et Spes*, for he goes on to describe that list as a number of examples of acts which *per se* and in themselves are always wrong by reason of their object, independently of circumstances (*VS*, 80). Now, clearly, what distinguishes the deportation of the dangerous *persona non grata* referred to above from the kinds of deportation that the writers of *Gaudium et Spes* presumably had in mind when they included that item in their list are circumstances and intention. If, therefore, someone were to say in exasperated tones to a critic of *Veritatis Splendor* that she (the critic) knows precisely what the pope has in mind and should stop playing with words, the critic could reply that she would have presumed that she knew what the pope had in mind if he had not described deportation as always wrong, regardless of circumstances and intention. The fact that he has done so, however, appears to rule out interpretations like: 'The pope is obviously referring only to such and such a type of deportation.' After all, when the pope says that deliberate artificial contraception is wrong, he means that it is wrong in *all* cases. That is something we have heard from Vatican sources over and over again. If, therefore, he is applying the same kind of reasoning to deliberate deportation, we can only conclude that he must mean that *all* deportation is wrong, unless, of course, he and all the other people involved in the writing of the encyclical have simply not noticed that deportation is one of the items in the list.

Similar problems arise, however, with mutilation, another item in the same list of 'intrinsically evil' acts. Dictionary definitions of mutilation refer to cutting off or out, destroying the use of or rendering imperfect a limb or organ of the body of a human, an animal or whatever. Clearly, the pope is concerned here only with mutilation as applied to humans because the word appears in the list as one of a category of acts that violate the integrity of the human person. Does the pope really believe that all mutilation is wrong? If we take seriously his comments about circumstances and intentions, we are left with no alternative but to assume that he does, but it is difficult to see why he would make such a claim. In the words of C. Henry Peschke,

> Integrity of members is not an absolute value, as every Catholic theologian admits. It may and often even must be sacrificed (by amputation or mutilation) for the well-being of the whole body. The preservation of the whole organism is more important than the conservation of a part, which in most instances of such necessities anyway became useless because of illness. Nevertheless this principle of the part-for-the-whole (principle of totality) is not only applicable to sick organs, but also to perfectly healthy ones if by their sacrifice the life as a whole can be saved. Thus it would be allowed to cut off a foot caught in a railroad track if this is the only means to save one's life.[6]

This kind of thinking was used in 1930 by Pope Pius XI in his encyclical *Casti Connubii*. We also find it and the expression 'principle of totality' in various discourses of Pius XII. Now, whatever doubts may have been expressed regarding the usefulness of the principle of totality since 1930, the fact remains that most moralists, and, one imagines, all popes up to John Paul II have approved of certain forms of mutilating surgery in cases in which it is considered necessary. Surely, moreover, up to the time of the publication of *Veritatis Splendor*, all Roman Catholic authorities would have agreed that, in deciding which cases of mutilating surgery were justifiable, one needed to know the circumstances and the intention. Surgery which could not be thus justified would be classified as unnecessary mutilation. In view of the fact that John Paul II has himself undergone mutilating surgery and has shown no signs of wishing to repent of his cooperation in that activity, one assumes that he does, in fact,

---

6. C. Henry Peschke, *Christian Ethics, Volume II: A Presentation of Special Moral Theology in the Light of Vatican II* (Alcester and Dublin: C. Goodliffe Neale, 1978) 316.

approve of it. We are left with a puzzle.[7]

We could perhaps consider the possibility that the pope simply did not notice that mutilation was in the list from *Gaudium et Spes* when he decided to use that list as a number of examples of intrinsically evil acts. This oversight would, of course, be additional to his not having noticed deportation. Another possibility is that he had in mind rather limited meanings for these words, meanings which are not as wide as the dictionary definitions. Neither of these two possibilities, however, provides a totally satisfactory explanation of the aversion to circumstances and intentions that pervades the whole of chapter two. Besides, it might seem rather far-fetched to suggest that the pope had either not noticed the presence of or had changed the meaning of not just two words, but three. There is, however, at least one other problematical item in that list. Mutilation and deportation are not the only enigmas.

Equally puzzling is the claim that any kind of homicide is intrinsically evil, regardless of circumstances and intention. This would seem to be something of a departure from magisterial tradition. Usually we are told that the only kind of killing that is always wrong regardless of circumstances and intention is direct killing of the innocent. Killing of aggressors may, under certain circumstances, be permitted. Even indirect killing of the innocent has traditionally been allowed, moreover, where there is a proportionate reason. Thus, some indirect killing of noncombatants in wartime has been tolerated. Another example is that of indirect abortion, as in the case of a hysterectomy performed upon a pregnant woman suffering from cancer of the uterus. Moreover, it is well known that, in the *Catechism of the Catholic Church,* approval is given to the inflicting of capital punishment on offenders in extremely serious cases if other penalties do not suffice to

---

7. George E. Lobo notes that mutilation is often distinguished from surgery in general. "By mutilation is meant the excision, or equivalent destruction, of a part of the body, so that the function is destroyed. Thus removal of an eye or the amputation of a limb would be called mutilation, while excision of a piece of the skin for grafting would not be mutilation as no organ or organic function would be destroyed." Such a distinction would not, of course, help the pope's case very much, because his ban on mutilation would rule out all amputations, etc. Lobo, moreover, goes on to note that "the skin too has a definite function and the body cannot withstand its destruction beyond a certain amount. Hence the distinction is not of much medical or ethical consequence." *Current Problems in Medical Ethics: A Comprehensive Guide to Ethical Problems in Medical Practice* (Allahabad, India: St. Paul Publications, 1974) pp. 72-73.

defend human life against aggressors and to protect public order and security.[8]

When one finds in an encyclical what appears to be an amazing change in traditional teaching, a change that one believes is not intended by the pope, one does well to consider the possibility of a bad translation. The apparently official Latin version, however, has *cuiusvis generis homicidia*, which does not seem to be of much help. Arguing about how Cicero might have used *homicidium* is likely to be a useless exercise in the circumstances, given the fact that these words were written in the twentieth century - although some people are given to indulging in that kind of activity when discussing papal and Council documents. What we really need to know is the precise meaning intended by the compilers of the list. It could, of course, be claimed that, whatever may or may not have happened with regard to deportation and mutilation, where homicide is concerned we do have a case of changing or limiting the meaning of a word. Indeed, some readers may, at this point, be of the opinion that we would do well to return to the theme of the above story about Margaret and Tracy. Surely, they may think, it is obvious that what is being referred to is murder. That may well be the case, but it does not help us to solve the puzzle.

The word 'murder' designates *unjustified* homicide. The question we need to ask is: how can we judge whether or not a particular instance of homicide is justified? The answer to that question is, of course, that we can do so only by taking the circumstances and intention into account. What, then, is the pope saying here? Does he perhaps believe that proportionalists are of the opinion that unjustified acts can be justified? And is he therefore merely pointing out that unjustified killing cannot be justified? If this is the case, I can only say that I know of no proportionalist who is of the opinion that the unjustified can be justified. It is odd, moreover, that Pope John Paul should say that the acts listed are always wrong regardless of circumstances and intention when it is clear that, at least where homicide, mutilation and deportation are concerned, we can only decide upon the rightness or wrongness of a particular instance after having taken circumstances and intention into account. Perhaps he means that, after having decided that a particular act is unjustified, we cannot then claim that it is in fact justified because of some other circumstances. That, however,

---

8. *Catéchisme de l'Église Catholique* (Paris: Mame/Plon, 1992) pp. 463-464.

would be a very strange claim to make. Surely it is possible, in a particular case, for us to have made a mistake in our judgment of the morality of an act precisely because we failed to take certain circumstances into account. Now that we have been made aware of those additional circumstances, we must take them into account, and perhaps change our original judgment.

It might be suggested, at this point, that the use of this list from *Gaudium et Spes* as a number of examples of intrinsically evil acts was simply a mistake on the part of the pope and his advisers. Perhaps they did not examine the list in detail before deciding to include it in the encyclical as a list of intrinsically evil acts. Considering this possibility and ignoring the list, however, does not make the problems go away. Having cited the *Catechism of the Catholic Church* teaching that there are certain kinds of behavior which it is always wrong to choose, "because choosing them involves a disorder of the will, that is, a moral evil," the pope goes on to quote Aquinas's observation that, often, humans act with a good intention, but without spiritual gain, because they lack a good will. If, says Thomas, we take the case of someone robbing in order to feed the poor, we can say that, even though the intention is good, the uprightness of the will is lacking. "Consequently, no evil done with a good intention can be excused." The pope then adds that the reason why a good intention is not of itself sufficient and that a correct choice of actions is also needed is because the human act depends on its object. (*VS*, 78)

In view of what we have already seen that John Paul II goes on to say about circumstances as well as intention, there would seem to be a need for some clarification here. If we can take it that Aquinas was using the word 'robbing' - or its Latin equivalent - to mean unjustified taking of another's property without that person's permission, we can say that he was not necessarily condemning all Robin Hood type activity. Moreover, in view of what he writes elsewhere regarding private ownership, one would not expect him to do so. Surely it has long been a teaching of what we might call all 'mainstream' Christian churches that, in extreme cases, when the rich refuse to help the poor, the poor may take what they need from them without their permission. Sometimes it happens that the poor are too weak to do the taking themselves. It may therefore be necessary for somebody else - who, needless to say, does not have enough in his or her possession to satisfy the needs in question - to do the taking for them. The circumstances make an enormous difference here. The word 'robbery' is, of course, used to indicate open and forcible taking of what belongs to another person. The use of force is, undoubtedly, a complicating factor, but the fact remains that there could exist circumstances in which it would be necessary to use a minimum of force to obtain the required goods. Thomas and the pope would appear to be right in saying that intention alone is not enough to justify the act, but that does not alter the fact that, *in certain circumstances*, taking from the rich with the intention of giving to the poor may be justified.

It would seem useful at this point to refer again to McCormick's belief that all proportionalists would admit the existence of acts which are intrinsically evil from their object, provided all the morally relevant circumstances are included in the object. Surely that kind of thinking has always been accepted since apostolic times by just about all authorities in the Church where the taking of another's property is concerned, even if that precise vocabulary was not always used (i.e, circumstances included in the object). The pope, however, gives the impression that he is not bearing this traditional line of thinking in mind here. Moreover, he gives that impression in more than one place. Further on, again taking up the subject of acts that are intrinsically evil, he accepts that a good intention or particular circumstances could diminish the evil of them. Nevertheless, he insists, they could not remove it. That is because those acts are 'irremediably' evil acts. He then refers to St. Augustine classifying theft, fornication, and blasphemy as acts which are themselves sins. Who, asked Augustine, would dare to affirm that, if one did them for good motives, they would no longer be sins, and who would make the absurd suggestion that they would be justified sins? It follows from this, says the pope - apparently treating Augustine's admittedly rhetorical question as an affirmation - that circumstances or intentions can never transform an act which, by virtue of its object, is intrinsically evil, into one that is 'subjectively' good or defensible as a choice (*VS*, 81). A couple of things need to be said about this. First, the word 'theft' has to be treated like 'robbery'. If Augustine is using it (or, as in the case of Aquinas, its Latin equivalent) to mean unjustified taking of another person's property (perhaps secretly, as opposed to the case of robbery, which might indicate stealing openly and forcibly), theft can obviously not be justified. In order to be able to judge whether or nor a particular instance of taking another's property (secretly or otherwise) is justified, however, - dare I say it again, at the risk of becoming boring? - we need to know the morally relevant circumstances and the intention of the person doing the taking.

The second thing that needs to be said is that, so far, we have concerned ourselves only with the distinction between morally right and morally wrong activity. As we have seen, however, John Paul II refers to acts which are themselves sins and to subjectively good acts. Here again some clarification is needed. Let us suppose that Susan does something which she later sees, with the benefit of hindsight, was the wrong thing to do in the circumstances. At the time, she did it in good conscience. She was convinced that what she was doing was morally right. She did not therefore sin. Something similar can be said about very serious matters regarding which moral sensitivities are generally more developed now than they were some years ago. Apparently, for instance, many Catholics in the past - including popes - thought that granting freedom of worship to non-Catholic visitors in Catholic countries was wrong, and they behaved accordingly. To our way of looking at things, with our sensitivities and, dare we say it, better reasoning on the subject, their behavior was abominable. What they did was clearly wrong, but the fact remains that, if they were convinced that what they were doing was right, they did not sin. The same can be said about St. Thomas More being involved in the execution of Protestants or about St. Bernard preaching the Second Crusade, again assuming that the two men in question sincerely believed at the time that what they were doing was morally right. In short, to talk about acts as sins, without taking persons fully into account is misleading.

NB.

Universal and Unchanging Moral Norms

Prostitution and trafficking in women and children are included in the list borrowed from *Gaudium et Spes*. Apart from this, there is not much mention of sexual matters in the second chapter of *Veritatis Splendor*, although there is a brief reference to contraception in a paragraph containing a quote from *Humanae Vitae* (*VS*, 81). It occurred to me more than once, however, whilst ploughing through the second chapter, that the description of what we might call various non-sexual actions as intrinsically evil regardless of circumstances and intention was perhaps made chiefly in order to strengthen the more frequently heard - though not necessarily understood - teachings regarding the intrinsically evil status of certain sexual acts which, in magisterial literature are classified as unnatural. If that is the case, the exercise would seem to have been a failure, because, in widening the list of intrinsically evil acts, the pope appears to have denied the possibility of justified surgery, justified homicide, justified deportation and justified taking of another person's property without that person's permission.

Some so-called 'traditionalist' moral theologians[9] apparently claim that papal teaching regarding artificial contraception cannot be changed because, they believe, it is intolerable or impossible that the Church could have been wrong for such a long period of time regarding such an important issue.[10] In spite of the fact that official teaching regarding other very important matters, such as slavery and religious liberty, was wrong for a very long period and was then changed, it is possible, one imagines, that the pope and his advisers were influenced by this kind of thinking when making claims in *Veritatis Splendor* concerning intrinsically evil acts, and were merely trying to strengthen their position by widening the spectrum of such acts. In fact, in the third chapter, there is a section in which the pope refers to the Church's "firmness in defending the universal and permanent validity of the precepts prohibiting intrinsically evil acts" (*VS*, 95). Further on he talks about "universal and unchanging moral norms" (*VS*, 96).

As a result of our analysis of some of the items listed in chapter two of the encyclical, we might, perhaps, be inclined to feel that, in trying to preserve teachings about some acts being intrinsically evil - perhaps principally the one's concerning so-called 'unnatural' sexual activity - the pope has, in fact, although, one imagines, unintentionally, changed a few things regarding teachings about killing, mutilation, deportation and the taking of other people's property. We could, however, and, it seems to me, should go more deeply than this into the matter of apparently unchanging and unchangeable norms.

---

9. Some may feel that this expression is used rather loosely nowadays in view of the fact that some of the leading 'traditionalists' are philosophers who have apparently not had any formal training in theology.

10. This was the view of the authors of the so-called 'minority report' of the Pontifical Commission for the Study of Population, Family and Birthrate. They claimed that the Roman Catholic Church could not change its teaching regarding the wrongness of such behavior because it could not have erred so atrociously and for such a long time regarding so serious a matter which imposed very heavy burdens on people. A 'traditionalist' line is taken by Germain Grisez and John C. Ford when they discuss this report in an article entitled "Contraception and the Infallibility of the Ordinary Magisterium," *Theological Studies* 39 (1978) 258-312.

Although I am inclined to disagree with what John Paul II has written regarding deportation, I am nonetheless pleased that, since the time of Pope Benedict XIV, there has been a change in papal teaching regarding this 'unchanging' norm. In 1751, Benedict wrote an encyclical concerning Jews and Christians living in the same place. It was addressed to the Primate, Archbishops and Bishops of the Kingdom of Poland. Therein, Benedict refers approvingly to one of his predecessors thus:

> Innocent IV,..., in writing to St. Louis, King of France, who intended to drive the Jews beyond the boundaries of his kingdom, approves of this plan since the Jews gave very little heed to the regulations made by the Apostolic See in their regard: "Since We strive with all Our heart for the salvation of souls, We grant you full power by the authority of this letter to expel the Jews, particularly since We have learned that they do not obey the said statutes issued by this See against them."[11]

Another item in the list borrowed by John Paul II from *Gaudium et Spes* and deemed intrinsically evil is "physical and mental torture and attempts to coerce the spirit" (*VS*, 80). Again I am pleased that John Paul II has chosen not to conform to the teaching of at least one of his predecessors regarding this matter. In 1252, in his Bull *Ad Extirpanda*, one of the popes referred to above, Innocent IV, permitted that heretics be tortured (barring amputation and death) so that they might reveal their own wrongdoing and even so that they might accuse others, as was already the case with thieves and marauders. This 'unchanging' norm has changed more than once. A few centuries before the time of Innocent IV - in 866, to be precise - Pope Nicholas I wrote a letter to the Bulgars in which he told them that neither divine nor human law admitted beating people in order to force confessions out of them.[12]

Even regarding the subject of homicide, the pope cannot fall back on an unchanging papal tradition. Pope Leo X condemned Martin Luther's claim

---

11. Benedict XIV, *A Quo Primum*, June 14, 1751. Translation as in Claudia Carlen, *The Papal Encyclicals 1740-1878* (New York: McGrath, 1981) 43.

12. For a longer treatment of this subject, see Francesco Compagnoni, "Capital Punishment and Torture in the Tradition of the Roman Catholic Church," *Concilium* 120 (1979) 39-53.

that it is against the will of the Holy Spirit to burn heretics at the stake.[13] *NB!* Of course, it might be claimed that there is development in papal teaching and that, where there is disagreement between popes, the faithful should follow the teaching of the more recent pontiff. Such a way of dealing with matters, however, would lead to serious difficulties where torture, for instance, is concerned, in view of the fact that the teaching of Innocent IV on the matter, to which we referred above, came nearly four centuries after the far superior teaching of Nicholas I.[14]

Clarifying the Issues

From what is said in the "Introduction" to *Veritatis Splendor*, one gains the impression that the pope fears there is an 'anything goes' mentality abroad in the Church. There may well be some people in the ranks of Catholicism who have such a mentality, and the pope undoubtedly does well to be concerned about them and about the influence they may have on others. Since the publication of the encyclical, many people, not all of them Catholics, have applauded his stance in this regard. John Paul II, however, seems to be of the opinion that the existence of the 'anything goes' mentality or at least something not too far removed from it is linked to the ideas promoted by certain moral theologians. Among them, it appears, the pope includes the group often referred to as proportionalists. *NB!* In view of the fact that a large percentage of the leading moral theologians in the Roman Catholic Church fall into that category, this is a most amazing state of affairs.

Pope John Paul notes that, as part of an effort to work out a rational morality, "there exist *false solutions, linked in particular to an inadequate understanding of the object of moral action*" (*VS*, 75). He then goes on to discuss at some length, as we have seen, the notion of intrinsically evil acts. A good deal of ink has been used up in writings on this matter over the last twenty five years or so. Although I have read a good deal of that literature, however, I had never, before setting eyes on *Veritatis Splendor*,

---

13. See *Denzinger-Schönmetzer* (ed. 32) 1483/773.

14. For a longer and more detailed treatment of so-called traditional teachings in the sphere of Christian ethics, see my forthcoming book: *Received Wisdom? Reviewing the Role of Tradition in Christian Ethics* (London: Geoffrey Chapman, 1994).

noticed any major disagreements between the holders of magisterial office and the revisionist moral theologians concerning such matters as mutilation, deportation, and the taking of another's property. Needless to say, there are some fairly major differences of opinion among Catholics concerning homicide. Some, for instance, declare themselves to be totally opposed to capital punishment. Some are total pacifists. Others - and here there may be a number of proportionalists - accept along with the holders of magisterial office that some killing may be legitimate but are not convinced that magisterial teaching on the subject deals adequately with all eventualities. It would seem, however, that, in spite of this, the main areas of dispute have been in the sphere of sexual morality.

There is, of course, real disagreement between John Paul II and the so-called proportionalists (and perhaps most other moral theologians) regarding the rightness or wrongness of deliberate artificial contraception and certain other activities which, in recent magisterial documents, have been classified as unnatural. The word disagreement is usually a fairly innocuous one. Unfortunately, however, it is replaced in much literature emanating from Vatican sources and in the writings of some so-called traditionalist scholars by the more emotive word 'dissent'. It is a short step from that word to others like 'disloyal' and 'unfaithful', and not such a long hop to 'promoters of an 'anything goes' mentality'. We all learned at an early age that we should look before leaping. Although leaping may be considered, on the whole, a potentially more dangerous activity than the other two just mentioned, it seems to me that there is also a good case for checking the ground ahead before hopping or even taking a step, especially in certain circumstances. To complete the picture, I should perhaps add that, if the hopping or stepping is being made backwards or sideways, the checking should be made in the appropriate direction. Additionally, one should not, perhaps, merely check the ground ahead, behind or to the side. One might also do well to be clear precisely why one wishes to engage in the hopping, stepping or jumping in the first place.

If John Paul II sincerely believes that popes are always necessarily right in what they say about matters of morality and that all disagreement with them regarding such issues amounts to an unhealthy dissent that could be accurately described as unfaithfulness to the Church, one can well under- stand why he should wish to bring those who disagree with him into line. There is ample evidence to show, however, that popes are not necessarily always right regarding moral matters. That much is evident from the instances of appalling errors on the part of popes which we have already had reason to note. Others could be listed. In 1452, for example, Nicholas V sent a Brief to King Alonso V of Portugal by means of which, with his Apostolic Authority, he granted to the latter full permission to invade, capture and subjugate Saracens, pagans and any others whom the pope described as unbelievers and enemies of Christ, and amongst other things, to reduce them into perpetual slavery. These grants were confirmed or renewed by Pope Calixtus III, Pope Sixtus IV and Pope Leo X. In 1493, Pope Alexander VI issued the Bulls *Eximiae Devotionis* and *Inter Caetera* in both of which he granted to the Spanish monarchy in respect to America those same favors, permissions, etc. that had already been granted to the Portuguese monarchy in respect to West Africa. In 1535 King Henry VIII of England was sentenced by Pope Paul III to the penalty of being exposed to capture and enslavement by the European Catholic princes. In 1548 that same pope granted permission to both clerics and lay people to own, buy and sell slaves in Rome. He also abrogated the privilege of the *conservatori* of that city to emancipate Christian slaves.[15]

Much more recently, in 1864, Pius IX promulgated his famous *Syllabus of Errors*. One of the condemned 'errors' listed therein is the proposition that it is no longer beneficial for the Catholic Church to be considered the only state religion to the exclusion of all other forms of worship. Another is that laws promulgated in some countries called Catholic wisely allow strangers to enjoy the public exercise of their own forms of worship.[16] It is well known by now that the views of Pius IX on these matters are very far removed from those expressed in *Dignitatis Humanae*, the Declaration on Religious Liberty of the Second Vatican Council. As far as I am aware, people like John Courtney Murray, who argued in favor of religious liberty before the change in official teaching came about, are not now referred to as dissenting theologians or as people who were unfaithful to the traditional teachings of the Roman Catholic Church. Now it is abundantly clear that many present day moral theologians are of the opinion that magisterial teaching regarding certain matters in the sphere of sexual morality is

---

15. For these details regarding slavery and the papacy I am indebted to the work of John F. Maxwell, *Slavery and the Catholic Church* (London: Barry Rose Publishers, 1975).

16. Pius IX, *Syllabus*, 77 and 78.

wrong, just as the teachings of Pius IX regarding religious liberty were
wrong. It does not necessarily follow from this that they are unfaithful to
the Church. They merely disagree with John Paul II, just as, I am sure,
both they and the pope disagree with the teachings of Innocent IV, Nicholas
V, Calixtus III, Sixtus IV, Paul III, Alexander VI, Leo X and Pius IX
regarding various issues already referred to here. Surely, therefore, we
should be indulging in dialogue rather than condemnation of certain ways
of thinking, especially when those ways of thinking are misunderstood or
malpresented in papal documents.

We live in a very complicated world, in which it is not always easy to be
sure that a certain course of action is the right one and that another is
wrong. There are times when reasonable and very good people differ in
their opinions. It is not necessarily the case that those who disagree with
someone who is convinced that he or she is right are promoting an
'anything goes mentality', even if the someone concerned is a pope. The
fact is that we still have many areas of uncertainty to deal with and that
we still have a lot of struggling to do together. It should not be so very
difficult for all of us to admit that there are areas of uncertainty and to
embrace dialogue without condemnation as part of the struggle. Besides,
it is often a very pleasant experience, as a result of open and honest
dialogue to arrive at a point where one can say at last: 'Now I know
precisely what you mean.'

Participation - Subordination:
(The Image of) God in *Veritatis Splendor*

Jan Jans

The first time I went through the text of *Veritatis Splendor*, my attention was particularly drawn by a reference to Saint Bonaventure in nr. 58. In discussing the judgment of conscience, the encyclical first wants to make clear that conscience is a witness of human faithfulness or unfaithfulness with regard to the law (*VS*, 57). Next, *Veritatis Splendor* adds to the importance of the interior dialogue within the person, that conscience is also a dialogue between human persons and God. The reason for this is that God is the author of the law. The encyclical then quotes Saint Bonaventure, who teaches that

> Conscience is like God's herald and messenger; it does not command things on its own authority, but commands them as coming from God's authority, like a herald when he proclaims the edict of the king. This is why conscience has binding force.

From this, *Veritatis Splendor* concludes that conscience is the witness of God, calling humankind to obedience.

Veritatis Splendor, as is quite clear from its "Introduction" on, is written to react against "the spread of numerous doubts and objections of a human and psychological, social and cultural, religious and even properly theological nature, with regard to the Church's moral teaching" (*VS*, 4). Among the topics on which dissent has caused a crisis according to the encyclical, is also the proper relationship between faith and morality:

> Also, an opinion is frequently heard which questions the intrinsic and unbreakable bond between faith and morality, as if membership in the Church and her internal unity were to be decided on the basis of faith alone, while in the sphere of morality a pluralism of opinions and of kinds of behavior could be tolerated, these being left to the judgment of the individual subjective conscience or to the diversity of social and cultural contexts (*VS*, 4).

In the third chapter of the encyclical, the consequences of the separation of faith from morality are spelled out as follows: "This separation represents one of the most acute pastoral concerns of the Church amid today's growing secularism, wherein many, indeed too many, people think and live 'as if God did not exist'" (*VS*, 88). Given this problematic situation, it should come as no surprise that *Veritatis Splendor* is dealing with the relationship between God and morality. The general direction of the proposed teaching is summed up in the definition that *Veritatis Splendor* offers of the theological science called 'moral theology':

> Moral theology is a reflection concerned with 'morality', with the good and the evil of human acts and of the person who performs them; in this sense it is accessible to all people. But it is also 'theology', inasmuch as it acknowledges that the origin and the end of moral action are found in the One who 'alone is Good' and who, by giving himself to man in Christ, offers him the happiness of divine life (*VS*, 29).

My own interest studying the precise way in which *Veritatis Splendor* deals with theology in the literal sense, i.e. the way in which the encyclical speaks of God, is shaped by a former investigation into the argumentative appeal to God in order to substantiate concrete moral norms. This investigation dealt with the 1987 Instruction *Donum Vitae*, issued by the Congregation for the Doctrine of the Faith. In it, I argued that "the theological part of *Donum Vitae's* moral argumentation operates with an image of God that portrays God as 'Lord of life' and 'Owner of certain rights in the gift of life' that effectively places God on the plane of categorical human activity".[1] The anthropomorphism present in *Donum Vitae* resulted in a hierarchy in the relationship between God and human beings, stressing the moral duty of obedience. This hierarchy itself was based on a specific re-interpretation of the teaching of *Humanae Vitae*, substantiating the moral value of the so-called connection between the two meanings of the conjugal act through the will of God, and therefore blaming as immoral the separation of the two meanings by human initiative. Although I am convinced that this re-interpretation was developed to support the conclusions of *Humanae Vitae*, it plays an important role in the

---

1. See "God or Man? Normative Theology in the Instruction *Donum Vitae*," *Louvain Studies* 17 (1992) 48-64, p. 50.

way *Veritatis Splendor* tries to resolve the ongoing moral theological controversy,[2] I will no longer pay attention to this here, but I will rather concentrate on the doctrine present in *Veritatis Splendor* on the general relationship between God and human beings with regard to morality as presented in the central chapter of the encyclical. My principal aim is to get a more precise idea of the actual teaching of the encyclical itself, therefore methodologically prescinding from questions regarding the interpretation of sources by *Veritatis Splendor*. Given the length and the complexity of the second chapter of *Veritatis Splendor*, I will first present an analysis of the relevant passages. In the second part, I will then venture upon an interpretation of the 'moral theology' of the encyclical.

Analysis

Although the proper noun 'Lawgiver' appears only twice in *Veritatis Splendor* to designate God (*VS*, 40 & 44), the category of 'law' and the related term 'commandments' are the central notions by which the significance of God for morality is put forward. In this analysis I will present the second chapter from this point of view, both by using direct quotes and paraphrases, each time referring to the corresponding number in the text of *Veritatis Splendor*.

Subtitled "The Church and the discernment of certain tendencies in present-day moral theology", the second chapter of *Veritatis Splendor* is divided in four sections, preceded by an introduction. Here, the pope lays out the aim of this chapter:

> It is my intention to state the principles necessary for discerning what is contrary to 'sound doctrine', drawing attention to those elements of the Church's moral teaching which today appear particularly exposed to error, ambiguity or neglect (*VS*, 30).

Among these is the question "what is freedom and what is its relationship to the truth contained in God's law?" (*VS*, 30). Since there can be no morality without freedom, the crucial issue will be to identify 'genuine freedom', and this in light of "certain tendencies in contemporary moral

---

2. See Jan Jans "Moraaltheologisch crisismanagement. Achtergronden en implicaties van de encycliek *Veritatis splendor*," *Tijdschrift voor Theologie* 34 (1994) 49-64.

theology ... (which) involve novel interpretations of the relationship of freedom to the moral law, human nature and conscience" (*VS*, 34).

Freedom and the Law

The first section of the second chapter then deals with the proper relation between freedom and law. Referring to the Book of Genesis, 2:16-17, *Veritatis Splendor* claims that although human beings possess an extremely far-reaching freedom, it is not unlimited:

> Revelation teaches that the power to decide what is good and what is evil does not belong to man, but to God alone. ... Freedom must halt before the 'tree of the knowledge of good and evil', for it is called to accept the moral law given by God (*VS*, 35).

In this, there is no trace of conflict between God's law and human freedom: "God, who alone is good, knows perfectly what is good for man, and by virtue of his very love proposes this good to man in the commandments" (*VS*, 35). However, those who disregard the dependence of human reason on Divine Wisdom, posit "a complete sovereignty of reason in the domain of moral norms regarding the right ordering of life in this world", and deny "the fact that the natural moral law has God as its author, and that man, by the use of reason, participates in the eternal law, which is not for him to establish" (*VS*, 36). Genuine freedom, then, is sharing in God's dominion which is to be exercised over the world and even over the human person: "God left man in the power of his own counsel" (*VS*, 38 & 39). The encyclical accepts the rightful autonomy of practical reason, which draws its own truth and authority from the eternal law. But,

> Were this autonomy to imply a denial of the participation of the practical reason in the wisdom of the divine Creator and Lawgiver, or were it to suggest a freedom which creates moral norms ... this sort of alleged autonomy would contradict the Church's teaching on the truth about man (*VS*, 40).

Now, since human freedom and God's law intersect, obedience to God cannot be set equal with heteronomy, a form of alienation. On the contrary, genuine moral autonomy might be expressed by the category of theonomy:

"man's free obedience to God's law effectively implies that human reason and human will participate in God's wisdom and providence" (*VS*, 41). Referring to Saint Thomas Aquinas, *Veritatis Splendor* next defines natural law: "... the light of natural reason whereby we discern good from evil, which is the function of the natural law, is nothing else but an imprint on us of the divine light" (*VS*, 42). Quoting the Second Vatican Council, it is stated that "God has enabled man to share in (t)his divine law, and hence man is able under the gentle guidance of God's providence increasingly to recognize the unchanging truth" (*VS*, 43). Again, it is through reason and its natural knowledge of God's eternal law, that persons are shown the right direction for action:

> In this way God calls man to participate in his own providence, since he desires to guide the world - not only the world of nature but also the world of human persons - through man himself, through man's reasonable and responsible care. The natural law enters here as the human expression of God's eternal law (*VS*, 43).

Again referring to the Thomistic doctrine of natural law, this time in the way it was used by Leo XIII, the encyclical stresses "the essential subordination of reason and human law to the Wisdom of God and to his law" (*VS*, 44). The divine Lawgiver constitutes a higher reason: "'The prescription of human reason could not have the force of law unless it were the voice and the interpreter of some higher reason to which our spirit and our freedom must be subject'" (*VS*, 44). This force of law is further explained as "its authority to impose duties, to confer rights and to sanction certain behavior" (*VS*, 44), something which would be impossible if humans were to be their own supreme legislator. *Veritatis Splendor* illustrates this 'reason enlightened by Divine Revelation and by faith' first by pointing to the law and the commandments given to Israel on mount Sinai, and next by recalling that the Church received the gift of the 'New Law'. However, "these and other useful distinctions always refer to that law whose author is the one and same God and which is always meant for man" (*VS*, 45). It would therefore be a mistake to see the different ways God is acting in history as mutually exclusive: God's plan "poses no threat to man's genuine freedom; on the contrary, the acceptance of God's plan is the only way to affirm that freedom" (*VS*, 45).

From the non-contradiction between God's law and human freedom, *Veritatis Splendor* draws to counter the alleged conflict between freedom and nature: "Other moralists ... frequently conceive of freedom as somehow in opposition to or in conflict with material and biological nature over which it must progressively assert itself" (*VS*, 46). The common mistake of these moralists according to the encyclical is to overlook the created dimension of nature and to misunderstand its integrity. Referring to God who "made man as a rationally free being; he left him 'in the power of his own counsel' and he expects him to shape his life in a personal and rational way" (*VS*, 47), they loose sight of the "correct relationship existing between freedom and human nature, and in particular *the place of the human body in questions of natural law*" (*VS*, 48, emphasis in original). Since the human person is in truth a unity - *corpore et anima unus* - reason and free will are linked with bodily faculties. This leads the encyclical to the conclusion that "the person, by light of reason and the support of virtue, discovers in the body the anticipatory signs, the expression and the promise of the gift of self, in conformity with the wise plan of the Creator", and "that reason grasps the specific moral value of certain goods towards which the person is naturally inclined" (*VS*, 48). This culminates in 'the true meaning of the natural law': it cannot be conceived of as simply a set of norms on the biological level; "'rather it must be defined as the rational order whereby man is called by the Creator to direct and regulate his life and actions and in particular make use of his own body'" (*VS*, 50, quoting *Donum Vitae*).

The final part of this first section of the second chapter of *Veritatis Splendor* deals with the repercussions of the alleged conflict between freedom and nature, namely the denial of both universality and immutability of the natural law. Once "the perception of the universality of the moral law on the part of reason" (*VS*, 51) is obscured, and the "immutability of the natural law itself" is questioned, the further step is taken to doubt "the existence of 'objective norms of morality' valid for all people of the present and the future, as for those of the past" (*VS*, 53). While admitting that "there is a need to seek out and to discover the most adequate formulation for universal and permanent moral norms in the light of different cultural contexts", this interpretation of the truth of the moral law is proper to the Magisterium: "the norms expressing that truth remain valid in their substance, but must be specified and determined '*eodem sensu eademque sententia*' in the light of historical circumstances by the Church's

Magisterium, whose decision is preceded and accompanied by the work of interpretation and formulation characteristic of the reason of individual believers and of theological reflection" (*VS*, 53).

Conscience and Truth

The second section of the chapter is titled "Conscience and truth". According to *Veritatis Splendor*, moral conscience is the 'place' where "the relationship between man's freedom and God's law is most deeply lived out" (*VS*, 54). However, the genuine normative significance is lost in the so-called creative understanding of moral conscience, based by its proponents on the value of conscience as "'the sanctuary of man, where he is alone with God whose voice echoes within him'" (*VS*, 55). Here, conscience is no longer a 'judgment', but a 'decision', to be made 'autonomously' by individual persons in particular cases. A further step along this road is to separate, or even to oppose, the teaching of a precept - valid in general - and the normative decision of the individual conscience. However, "these approaches pose a challenge to the very identity of the moral conscience in relation to human freedom and God's law" (*VS*, 56).

Referring to Saint Paul, the encyclical next indicates conscience as 'witness': "conscience in a certain sense confronts man with the law, and thus becomes a 'witness' for man: a witness with regard to his own faithfulness or unfaithfulness with regard to the law" (*VS*, 57). Being hidden in the heart of the person, conscience is therefore an interior dialogue, but not just a dialogue within the person, but also a dialogue between persons and God, the author of the law. Quoting Saint Bonaventure who holds that conscience does not command on its own authority but on God's - just like a herald who is proclaiming the edict of a king - *Veritatis Splendor* concludes that "conscience is the witness of God himself, whose voice and judgment penetrate the depths of man's soul, calling him *fortiter and suaviter* to obedience" (*VS*, 58). Again in reference to Saint Paul, the notion of 'conflicting thoughts' clarifies the precise nature of conscience:

> It is a moral judgment about man and his actions, a judgment either of acquittal or of condemnation, according as human acts are in conformity or not with the law of God written on the heart (*VS*, 59).

Since conscience is a judgment of actions, it can rightly be called a practical judgment: "it is the application of the law to a particular case; ... it formulates moral obligation in the light of the natural law" (*VS*, 59). By this, it should be clear that conscience does not establish the law or have the capacity to decide what is good and evil: "rather it bears witness to the authority of the natural law and of practical reason with reference to the supreme good, whose attractiveness the human person perceives and whose commandments he accepts" (*VS*, 60). Finally, given the link between freedom and truth, which is made manifest in the judgment of conscience reflecting the truth about the good, the responsibility and maturity of conscience "are not measured by the liberation of the conscience from objective truth, in favor of an alleged autonomy in personal decisions, but, on the contrary, by an insistent search for truth, and by allowing oneself to be guided by that truth in one's actions" (*VS*, 61).

However, because conscience is not exempt from the possibility of error, *Veritatis Splendor* pays special attention to the necessity of seeking the truth. After recalling the doctrine on erroneous conscience and the possibility of invincible ignorance, the encyclical also warns about conscience "compromising its dignity when it is culpably erroneous" (*VS*, 63) by showing little concern for what is true and good. In response to this, the encyclical stresses the need for continuous formation of conscience, both by knowledge of God's law in general and by developing "a sort of 'connaturality' between man and the true good" (*VS*, 64). Christians are furthermore reminded that they "have a great help for the formation of conscience in the Church and her Magisterium", the authority of which in no way undermines the freedom of conscience of Christians, because "the Magisterium does not bring to the Christian conscience truths which are extraneous to it" (*VS*, 64).

Applications

The remaining sections of the second chapter of *Veritatis Splendor* are to an important degree an application of the doctrine developed in the sections dealing with freedom, God's law, conscience and truth. Their analysis from the point of view of the relationship between God and human beings with regard to morality can therefore be much shorter. First, the encyclical deals with the proper relation between 'fundamental choice and specific kinds of behavior'. If freedom is also "a decision about oneself and a setting of one's own life for or against the Good, for or against the Truth and ultimately for or against God" (*VS*, 65), then this capacity "is actually exercised in the particular choices of specific actions, through which man deliberately conforms himself to God's will, wisdom and law" (*VS*, 67). In opposition to some tendencies that according to *Veritatis Splendor* lead to a separation between fundamental choice and obedience of the moral law and God's commandments, the encyclical holds that "with every freely committed mortal sin, man offends God as the giver of the law and as a result becomes guilty with regard to the entire law" (*VS*, 68). *Veritatis Splendor* adds that mortal sin does not only exist in the rejection of God, God's law and covenant of love by an act of fundamental option, but also "in every act of disobedience to God's commandments in a grave matter" (*VS*, 70).

The final section of the second chapter focuses on 'the moral act'. *Veritatis Splendor* recalls that "the relationship between man's freedom and God's law, which has its intimate and living center in the moral conscience, is manifested and realized in human acts" (*VS*, 71). The morality of such acts - expressing and determining the goodness or evilness of the individual who performs them - is defined by their rational, free, conscious and deliberate ordering towards God. If, therefore,

> the object of the concrete action is not in harmony with
> the true good of the person, the choice of that action
> makes our will and ourselves morally evil, thus putting
> us in conflict with our ultimate end, the supreme good,
> God himself (*VS*, 72).

Reviewing the so-called 'sources of morality', the encyclical then opposes as not faithful to the Church's teaching, theories which "believe they can justify as morally good, deliberate choices of kinds of behavior contrary to the commandments of the divine and natural law" (*VS*, 76). In contrast, *Veritatis Splendor* teaches that "the primary and decisive element for moral judgment is the object of the human act, which establishes whether it is capable of being ordered to the good and to the ultimate end, which is God" (*VS*, 79). As a consequence, acts which by reason of their object are "'incapable of being ordered' to God, because they radically contradict the good of the person made in his image" (*VS*, 80) are according to the encyclical rightfully termed 'intrinsically evil', leading to prohibitive norms which are binding without exception.

Commentary

In order to understand the way God is present in the teaching of *Veritatis Splendor*, I suggest to consider the possibility of a certain - uneasy - dualism or ambiguity. The two keywords that can be used to bring this into focus are *participation* on the one hand, and *subordination* on the other. From the analysis outlined above, this can be systematized as follows: participation is present in categories like sharing, autonomy, intersection, theonomy, (gentle) guidance, recognition, discernment, imprint, responsible care, gift, shaping, calling, dialogue, attractiveness, acceptance, connaturality and confirmation; subordination is present in categories such as dependence, author - authority, dominion, obedience, higher reason, force of law, subjection, imposition and sanction.

The Power to Decide

Of course, *Veritatis Splendor* would claim that all of these categories express the relationship between God and human beings and should be kept together, which is the very case favored by the encyclical itself. Over against this, I would like to ask to what extent this is possible in a legitimate way. My main point here is the problematic nature of the image of God present in the key-passages used to refute so-called 'tendencies in present-day moral theology'. After identifying these tendencies as being "at one in lessening or even denying *the dependence of freedom on truth*" (*VS*, 34, emphasis in original), this dependence is forcefully illustrated by the "most authoritative expression found in the words of Christ: 'You will know the truth, and the truth will set you free' (Jn 8:32)" (*VS*, 34). Immediately following this, in the opening sentences of the section dealing with 'freedom and law', *Veritatis Splendor* goes on to quote from Genesis: "You may eat freely of every tree of the garden; but of the tree of knowledge of good and evil you shall not eat, for in the day that you eat of it you shall die" (*VS*, 35). Leaving aside the question whether Adam and Eve would factually die (in which case the prohibition is meant to protect them), or if they would have to die (meaning the prohibition is a threat), it still strikes me as rather strange that upon the word of Jesus recommending knowledge of the truth, the readers of *Veritatis Splendor* seem to have to ask themselves whether 'the knowledge of good and evil' is to be included in this.

However, this is not the point that the encyclical wants to make, since it continues not on the theme of knowledge but shifts towards 'the power to decide': "With this imagery, Revelation teaches that *the power to decide what is good and what is evil does not belong to man, but to God alone*" (*VS*, 35, emphasis in original). The real conflict according to *Veritatis Splendor* is to be found between "doctrines (which) would grant to individuals or social groups the right *to determine what is good or evil*" in which "freedom ... would actually amount to an *absolute sovereignty*" (*VS*, 35, emphasis in original) and God's exclusive power to decide what is good and what is evil. Again, the section dealing with 'conscience and truth', referring to "the tendency - ... to exalt freedom almost to the point of idolatry - (which leads) to a *'creative' understanding of moral conscience*" (*VS*, 54) counters this form of atheism by remembering that

> Conscience is not an independent and exclusive capacity to decide what is good and what is evil. Rather, there is profoundly imprinted upon it a principle of obedience vis-à-vis the objective norm which establishes and conditions the correspondence of its decisions [*sic*] with the commands and prohibitions which are at the basis of human behavior (*VS*, 60, quoting John Paul II).

Based on this, and notwithstanding the clear presence and the continued insistence upon 'participatory' language and categories, the two sections of the second chapter on freedom and conscience nevertheless propose a hierarchy in the relation between God and persons, as becomes clear from the already mentioned quotes from Leo XIII (the essential subordination of reason and human law; the higher reason to which our spirit and our freedom must be subject) and from Saint Bonaventure (the commandments of conscience are not on its own authority but on God's, conscience being like a herald only proclaiming the edict of the king). This hierarchy is in the last resort based upon the antagonism 'not human persons, but God': God alone - not the human person - has the power to decide what is good and evil, and since God is the Author of the Law and the Commandments these are to be accepted and submitted to. Of course, one might argue that such moral voluntarism must not in and of itself mean heteronomy, in which the moral life is "subject to the will of something all-powerful, absolute, extraneous to man and intolerant of his freedom" (*VS*, 41). *Veritatis Splendor* first claims that "God, who alone is good, knows perfectly what is good for man, and by virtue of his very love proposes this good to man in the commandments" (*VS*, 35). Later it concludes that "the Magisterium does not bring to the Christian conscience truths which are extraneous to it; rather it brings to light the truths which it ought already to possess" (*VS*, 64). I will briefly return to this in my conclusion, but first I wish to elaborate on the antagonism just mentioned.

A Hermeneutical Key

Veritatis Splendor, as the text of the encyclical itself notes in reference to a letter written in 1987 (*VS*, 5), took a long time to compose and prepare for promulgation. During this period, the pope delivered an address to the participants of the second international congress for moral theology, organized on the occasion of the twentieth anniversary of *Humanae vitae*.[3] I have already alluded to the importance of the re-interpretation developed in support of the conclusions of *Humanae Vitae*. In the address, given on November 12, 1988, John Paul II supported this re-interpretation in an unprecedented way. The address, which is nowhere referred to in *Veritatis Splendor*, can in my opinion be seen as a hermeneutical key for a better understanding of the whole of the encyclical. With regard to the morality of the norm upheld by *Humanae Vitae*, the pope claims that the teaching of *Humanae Vitae* is not invented by human beings, but inscribed by God's creative hand into the nature of the human person and confirmed in Revelation. Therefore, those who bring this norm into discussion refuse the obedience of their intelligence to God himself: they prefer the light of their own reason over against the light of Divine Wisdom. Consequently, the Christian doctrine of conscience also gets obscured, by accepting the idea that it is conscience which creates the moral norm. By this, humankind radically breaks the string of obedience to the holy will of the Creator. Conscience, to be sure, is not enlightened by its own created reason, but by the wisdom of the Word that created everything.

Although there is a great difference in tone and style between this address and *Veritatis Splendor*, the latter being much more nuanced in formulation, the parallels are obvious. Authentic moral commandments are not 'invented

---

3. John Paul II, "Non si può parlare di diligente ricerca della Verità se non si tiene conto di ciò che il Magistero insegna," *L'Osservatore Romano*, 13 Nov. 1988, 4; *A.A.S.* 81 (1989) 1206-1211; translated into French as: "La doctrine de la vérité," *L'Osservatore Romano* (Hebd. en langue française), 13 Dec. 1988, 8-9.

by human beings', but 'inscribed by the creator' and therefore to be accepted. Dissent comes down to the sin of hubris caused by the idolatry of freedom, and 'creative conscience' separates human persons from God. The theology behind both this address and *Veritatis Splendor*, although 'veiled' by the vocabulary of participation, ultimately comes down to 'who is in charge': God or human persons?

God as 'Lawgiver'

As I pointed out above, my interest is focused on the image of God behind the model of subordination. It should be clear that the discussion between the model of participation on the one hand and of subordination on the other, is not limited to the field of moral theology. Rather, the model used in moral theology, and especially so in efforts to substantiate concrete norms[4], is more or less revelatory of deeper positions held at the level of fundamental theology. The way in which the relation between God and human persons is understood follows most basically from the concept of revelation. For Christians, this ultimately comes down to the person of Jesus the Christ: how is God revealed in Jesus, and/or: how is Jesus the self-revelation of God? The history of christology testifies to the various ways developed to articulate this revealing relation, and the employment of - among others - the models of participation and subordination. Behind a concrete christology, there always is a substantiating image of God. The history of christological controversy also testifies, that not all of these christologies and their related *Gottesbilder* are mutually compatible.

Returning to the question of morality, the moral theological enterprise cannot 'economize' on the question of God's relation to human beings and the corresponding image of God.[5] Historically, the image of God portrayed as 'Lawgiver' plays an important role here, but it is certainly not free from ambiguity. Interpreted through a participatory christology, the law given by God is nothing other then the Law of Christ, and God's will an invitation to act according to the new life of grace which becomes a true possibility for those who co-participate in Jesus' relation towards God.

---

4. An example of this is the already mentioned Instruction *Donum Vitae*. See note 1.

5. See Klaus Demmer, *Moraltheologische Methodenlehre*, (Studien zur theologischen Ethik, 27; Freiburg i. Ue.: Universitätsverlag/ Freiburg i. Br. - Wien: Herder, 1989) pp. 74-77.

However, God's law can also be interpreted as the exemplification of a cosmic order, such that God's will appears to be a command or a set of commandments probably in conflict with human freedom. This second interpretation leads to the problem of heteronomy: God and humankind are standing over against each another in an antagonistic way, a state of conflict that can only be decided by the one who holds supreme power over good and evil. Therefore, morality becomes framed in the language of obedience: being only creatures, human beings have to obey the Author of creation.

It seems to me that, next to a rather pessimistic interpretation of the 'fallen state' of human nature, the core of the problem in this antagonism is situated in the defective attention given to the so-called analogy of being. The model of subordination becomes inevitable from the moment that God and human beings are proposed as acting on the same level of being. If, indeed, the freedom and creativity that human beings claim for themselves is considered to be to the detriment of God's sovereignty, then the only solution to solve 'demarcation disputes' and to maintain the proper hierarchy between God and man is to stress the force of God's law: "The force of law consists in its authority to impose duties, to confer rights and to sanction certain behavior" (*VS*, 44). However, the alleged conflict and the resulting need of subordination disappear once the requirements of the analogy of being are taken seriously, with the result that God and human beings are seen to be acting on different planes of being: "The difference may be seen as that between two oarsmen rowing a boat together and a sail driving a boat under the power of the wind".[6] As far as I can see, it is also this analogy of being which is operative in the theory of fundamental option, pointing out the difference - and of course the connection through participation in grace - between God as transcendental creator and human beings as categorical creatures.

Conclusion

Veritatis Splendor claims both that God only proposes in the commandments what is good for human persons and that the proper contribution of the Magisterium is to make visible those truths which

---

6. John Mahoney, *The Making of Moral Theology. A Study of the Roman Catholic Tradition*, (Oxford: Clarendon, 1987) p. 247.

Christian conscience already ought to know. If one takes this seriously, there can be no question of imposed morality or heteronomy. At the same time, if one equally takes seriously what *Veritatis Splendor* has to say on the "need to seek out and to discover the most adequate formulation for universal and permanent moral laws in the light of the different cultural contexts", namely that "the decision of the Church's Magisterium is preceded and accompanied by the work of interpretation and formulation characteristic of the reason of individual believers and of theological reflection" (*VS*, 53), then this amounts to a claim for the universality of the model of participation and the inadequacy of any notion of subordinate obedience. In addition, and pointing in the same direction, is the way the encyclical treats the topic of 'infallibility':

> The whole Church is called to evangelization and to the witness of a life of faith, by the fact that she has been made a sharer in the *munus propheticum* of the Lord Jesus through the gift of his Spirit. Thanks to the permanent presence of the Spirit of truth in the Church (cf. Jn 14:16-17), "the universal body of the faithful who have received the anointing of the holy one (cf. 1 Jn 2:20,27) cannot be mistaken in belief. It displays this particular quality through a supernatural sense of the faith in the whole people when, 'from the Bishops to the last of the lay faithful', it expresses the consensus of all in matters of faith and morals" (*VS*, 109, quoting *Lumen Gentium*).

It might finally come as no surprise that some of the present-day moral theologians whose work is 'evaluated' by *Veritatis Splendor*, see their own specific contribution to the discipline as ways to overcome the antagonism between God as ruling king and human beings as obedient servants, precisely because this antagonism conflicts with their understanding of both God as the transcendental mystery of involved love and the human person as categorical moral subject.[7] However, this anthropocentric turn - exempl-

7. See Josef Römelt, *Personales Gottesverständnis in heutiger Moraltheologie auf dem Hintergrund der Theologien von K. Rahner und H. U. von Balthasar* (Innsbrucker theologische Studien, 21; Innsbruck/Wien: Tyrolia, 1988) p. 23: "Die Moraltheologie (ist) auf dem Weg zur Überwindung der objektivistischen Deutung des sittlichen Anspruchs und des damit verbundenen Autoritätsdenkens und ist auf dem Weg zu der am Freiheitsvollzug des Menschen selbst ausgerichteten Auslegung des sittlichen Sollens". The moral theologians mentioned by Römelt in his study are Franz Böckle, Bruno Schüller, Klaus Demmer and Hans Rotter.

ified within this context in legitimate notions such as co-creator - no longer leaves room for the image of God as a ruling and competing moral authority, imposing a moral will through creation and the revelation of commandments. This also calls for a revision of some traditional understandings and interpretations of God's creative presence in the realm of 'nature', as well as a revaluation of the concrete norms following from this perspective. The tension over this revision, which is at the root of *Veritatis Splendor* itself, is in the last analysis a controversy over the image of God implied in the models of moral subordination versus moral participation. The fact that both of them are present in the encyclical does not prove that they can co-exist. To the extent that they are seen mutually to exclude one another, *Veritatis Splendor* could rather be interpreted as an occasion for taking up the task and the responsibility to further investigate and clarify the ways in which (an image of) God is - or rather should be - present in moral theology.[8]

---

8. See Marciano Vidal, "Die Moraltheologie als Dienst an der Sache des Menschen. Zur grundlegenden Orientierung unserer heutigen Moraltheologie," *Theologie der Gegenwart* 33 (1990) 3-19; and Klaus Demmer, *Gottes Anspruch denken. Die Gottesfrage in der Moraltheologie* (Studien zur theologischen Ethik, 50; Freiburg i. Ue.: Univ. verlag/ Freiburg i. Br. - Wien: Herder, 1993).

Index of Persons, Documents and Scriptural References in *Veritatis Splendor*[1]

Leon Derckx

Index of Persons

---

1. In the index of persons and documents, numbers in ordinary print refer to the paragraph numbers of the encyclical and numbers printed in italics refer to footnote numbers. In the index of scriptural references, ordinary numbers refer to paragraph numbers of the encyclical in which the text is quoted while numbers within parentheses indicate that only reference is given, without a quotation. There are no quotations of scripture in the footnotes.

Index of Documents

Index of Scripture Quotations and References

Jn 1:17	23
Jn 2:5	120
Jn 3:5	107
Jn 3:5-8	(25)
Jn 3:14-15	(14)
Jn 3:16-18	(118)
Jn 3:21	(24), 64
Jn 4:23	87
Jn 5:39	15
Jn 6:44	(19)
Jn 6:45	(19)
Jn 6:51-58	(21)
Jn 8:12	(19)
Jn 8:32	31, 34, 87
Jn 8:44	1
Jn 9:39-41	(63)
Jn 10:11-16	(19)
Jn 12:32	(87)
Jn 13:1	(14), 20
Jn 13:14-15	20
Jn 13:34-35	(15), 20
Jn 14:6	2, (19), (83), (88)
Jn 14:6-10	(19)
Jn 14:15	(119)
Jn 14:16-17	(109)
Jn 14:26	(25)
Jn 15:9	22
Jn 15:10	24
Jn 15:12	20
Jn 15:13	20, (50), 87
Jn 16:13	(19), (28)
Jn 18:37	87
Jn 18:38	(1)
Jn 19:34	(103)
Joel 2:3	(105)
Jos 24:14-25	(66)
Lev 19:2	10, (115)
Lev 26:12	10

Rom 8:21	(18)
Rom 8:29	45, (73)
Rom 9:1	(62)
Rom 10:4	15
Rom 10:10	(66)
Rom 12:1	107
Rom 12:2	62, 64, (64), 85
Rom 12-15	(26)
Rom 13:8-9	17
Rom 13:8-10	(13), (76)
Rom 16:26	(66)
Sir 15:14	(34), 38, 39
Sir 15:19-20	102
1 Thes 1:9	(1)
1 Thes 4:1	(28)
1 Thes 5:4-8	(88)
1 Tim 1:5	62
1 Tim 1:10	116
1 Tim 3:15	27
1 Tim 6:13	91
2 Tim 1:3	62
2 Tim 1:6	(109)
2 Tim 4:1-4	(114)
2 Tim 4:1-5	30
2 Tim 4:3	5, 29
Tit 1:10,13-14	(30)
Tit 2:1	(28)
Wis 2:12	(93)
Wis 7:22	(43)
Wis 8:11	(43)
Wis 18:4	(12)

Contributors

Joseph A. Selling, S.T.D., is professor of moral theology at the Katholieke Universiteit Leuven, Belgium. Address: St.-Michielsstraat 6, B-3000 Leuven.

Gareth Moore, S.T.L., M. Litt., is subprior and lector of Old Testament and Hebrew at Blackfriars, and a member of the Faculty of Theology, University of Oxford, England. Address: 64 St. Giles, Oxford OX1 3LY.

Louis Janssens, S.T.M., is professor emeritus of moral theology at the Katholieke Universiteit Leuven, Belgium. Address: Kardinaal Mercierlaan 95, B-3001 Heverlee.

Brian V. Johnstone, S.T.D., is professor of moral theology at the Accademia Alfonsiana, Rome, Italy. Address: Via Merulana, 31, C.P. 2458, I-00100 Roma.

Bernard Hoose, S.T.D., is professor of moral theology at Heythrop College, University of London, England. Address: Kensington Square, London, W8 5HQ.

Jan Jans, S.T.D., is a docent in moral theology at the Theologische Faculteit Tilburg, The Netherlands. Address: Academielaan 9, NL-5037 ET Tilburg.

Leon Derckx is a student-assistant at the Theologische Faculteit Tilburg, The Netherlands. Address: Academielaan 9, NL-5037 ET Tilburg.